Gut It · Cut It
Cook It

The Deer Hunter's Guide to
Processing & Preparing Venison

Eric Fromm & Al Cambronne

Published by

Krause Publications, a division of F+W Media, Inc.
700 East State Street • Iola, WI 54990-0001
715-445-2214 • 888-457-2873
www.krausebooks.com

Library of Congress Control Number: 2009923231

ISBN-13: 978-1-4402-0370-1
ISBN-10: 1-4402-0370-9

Designed by Kara Grundman
Edited by Corrina Peterson

Printed in China

ACKNOWLEDGEMENTS

First, we'd like to thank Al's wife, Jean Hedren. Thanks to her the photos in this book look great. She took many of them.

Second, we'd like to thank both our wives for their understanding and patience as we worked on this book. Thanks, too, for helping "gut, cut and cook" all that venison.

Thanks to my wife Julie's parents, Don and Carol, for the old-time "buck pole" photo. Thanks, too, to Julie's dad for helping obtain the buck shown in Chapter 15. Nice shot, Don! Finally, a special thanks to joyceimages.com for the photo of an old-time butcher shop.

Thanks to John and Shorty for the ag-tag hunts on your farms. Without those deer this book might not have been ready nearly as soon.

We'd like to thank Corrina Peterson, our Editor at Krause Publications. We're grateful for her guidance and patience as she shepherded this book through its final stages.

Finally, we'd like to thank Harris Andrews at Stoeger for having faith in us.

We have just as much faith in you, our readers. We know you'll do more than just skim this book for entertainment. Read it, study it, and then use it.

Let's get to work.

Table of Contents

FOREWORD

If you can clean your own fish, you can process your own venison.

You can do it. In this book we'll show you how— step by step—with simple, clear instructions that are easy to follow.

Let's be realistic though. This book won't make you an instant expert. The first few times it's going to take longer. We guarantee it. But we'll get you through this. Later, the job will get easier every time.

So, then… Why go to all the trouble?

Plenty of reasons. For now, let's just say that saving money, eating healthier and enjoying better-quality venison are only part of the story.

The biggest reason is something less tangible—that feeling you get from being just a little more self-reliant. There's something satisfying about doing the job yourself rather than paying someone else to do it for you.

Sure you can get a taste of that same feeling by canning your own tomatoes, building your own deck or remodeling your own bathroom. But this is different. This is, as they used to say, "making meat."

There's something satisfying about knowing you've done it all yourself—from pulling the trigger to washing the dishes. Plus, you'll know exactly where that venison has been and how it's been handled every step of the way. Since you know that you and your family will be eating it, no one is going to do the job more carefully than you will.

Is it going to be effortless? No, not even after you've done it a hundred times.

Is it worth it? Absolutely, even the very first time.

If you can clean your own fish, you can process your own venison.

INTRODUCTION

It's true: Sometimes you really can judge a book by its cover.

As you may have already noticed, you can open this book and lay it out flat. Later, you'll be able to refer to it while you're skinning and butchering your first few deer. We've written a book that we hope will get used and get bloody.

Sure, you'll want to read this book before you go hunting and bring back a deer. When you're done, you may even want to study parts of it a second and third time. But we didn't write this book so you could read it by the fireside and pass a winter's evening.

This Book is Different.

This book is different, and its cover and binding are only the beginning. At every step of the way, we'll give you the support and guidance you need—even if you're doing this the very first time. If you've already done this a few times, you'll still learn how to do the job more efficiently. And even if you've already processed dozens of deer, you'll still come across a few ideas that can make the job easier next time around.

There are already plenty of books out there about hunting, and there are also plenty of cookbooks. If you like, buy a few of those books too. But there's a lot that has to happen in between making your shot and making your dinner.

That's where this book comes in. We're going to:

- **Show you the step-by-step details.** We'll give supportive tips and guidance every step of the way.

- **Focus on the details that matter most.** Other books devote only a few pages to the practical details of field-dressing, skinning and butchering. This book is different; that's where we'll spend nearly all of our time. No recipes, no hunting stories, and no history of deer hunting over the last 50,000 years. We promise.

- **Begin at the beginning.** We'll walk you through the important preparation steps that you'll want to take before you head out into the woods.

- **Tell you and show you.** Along with simple, clear explanations, we've included plenty of photos that show you how to complete each step.

So study up ahead of time and feel free to read this book when you're relaxing by the fireside in your easy chair. But we think you'll enjoy it most when you have a knife in one hand and a deer carcass in the other.

Meet the Authors: Two Different Perspectives

In this book you'll get expert guidance from a team that also understands the challenges you face as a learner.

Eric is an avid hunter, trapper and outdoorsman who works for the USDA as a wildlife specialist. Most of his work involves wolves and bears. When Eric was six years old, his uncle began teaching him how to process wild game. Growing up, he also helped butcher steers and a few hogs every fall. Later he worked for an outfitter at an elk camp in Colorado. He's hunted the West, the Midwest and Canada. Over the years he's processed elk, caribou, bears and hundreds of deer.

The voice you'll hear throughout the book is me, Al. I'm a freelance writer, photographer and instructional designer. Although I've spent a lot of time outdoors, most of it involved paddling, fishing, hiking, skiing or running. As a kid I did a lot of plinking and a little target shooting, but somehow I didn't take up hunting until much later. When I did, my friend Eric coached me a little on the hunting. Then he showed me how to skin and butcher my first few deer. That got the two of us thinking about this book.

I've spent most of my career creating training that helps people do their jobs better. Some projects involved training in sales, management or interpersonal skills; others involved more technical, process-related skills—kind of like this one.

Eric is an expert at gutting, cutting and cooking; my forté is helping people learn new skills. For you, that's good news. Get ready for some hands-on experiential learning.

Your Deer May Vary

If you look closely at the photos in this book, you'll see that every deer is different. Some are lean and others have lots of fat to trim away. Some deer are large and others are small.

We wrote this book to help you learn or perfect a skill—not to brag about our own skill as hunters. We've used a variety of deer for these photos. One relatively small doe stars in several photos. Because the carcass was so lean, it's easier than usual to see the different muscle groups.

Not all deer are huge. We'll tell you more about that later. But if the same cuts of meat look bigger on your deer than they do in these photos, good for you. Bon appetit!

We Know Some Great Recipes for Stir-Fries and Fajitas

This may not go perfectly the first few times. Don't sweat it. You won't ruin your venison by cutting it up wrong. This isn't a delicate surgical procedure; your deer is already dead.

If your roasts and steaks aren't evenly sliced and perfectly symmetrical, they'll still taste great. And remember, you'll be cutting some of the less tender cuts into chunks for burger, sausage or stew. They can be just about any shape and size; it doesn't matter.

Some of the prime cuts may not turn out perfectly either. Maybe you'll be left with some extra scraps and shreds of the very most prized, premium venison. No problem. They'll work great for stir-fries and fajitas. Sometimes we thaw a package of backstrap and then later, just as we turn on the stove, we slice it up into small strips for a stir-fry. You'll have already done that ahead of time.

Even if the very best cuts end up in shreds, it's OK. They'll be great for stir-fries and fajitas.

CHAPTER 1

What to Expect, and What's For Dinner

Photo courtesy of Jacob Edson

In this chapter, we'll give you a realistic idea of what to expect when field-dressing, skinning and butchering your deer. We'll also tell you more about why it's worth all the trouble, and why your wild game—especially venison—doesn't need to taste "gamey."

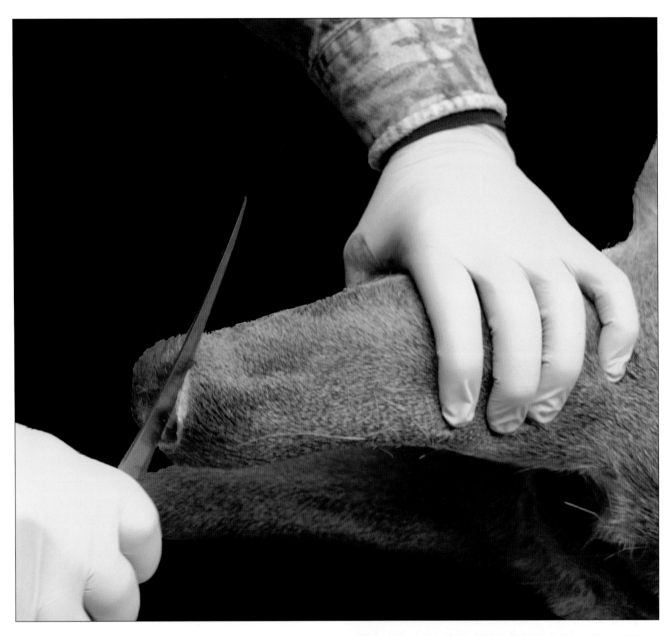

Once you get back home, you'll remove the deer's head and lower legs. (The exception, of course, would be if you've shot a buck and want to save its head and cape for the taxidermist.) Then you'll make a few cuts to expose the tendons in the deer's back legs and hang the deer up by a gambrel inserted through these tendons.

An Overview of the Process

Over the next several chapters, we'll explain the entire process in detail, step by step. For now, here is a quick overview of what's coming.

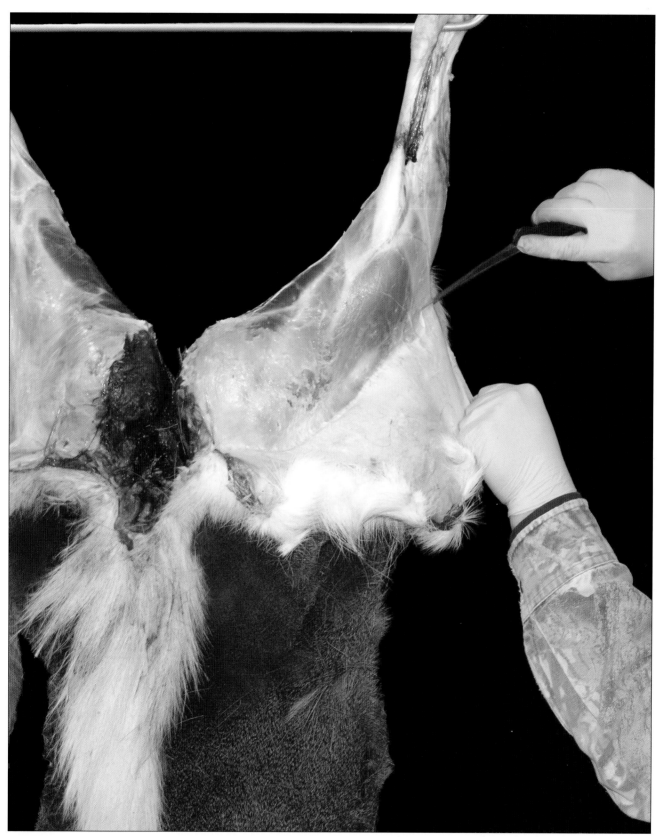

Next you'll skin the deer.

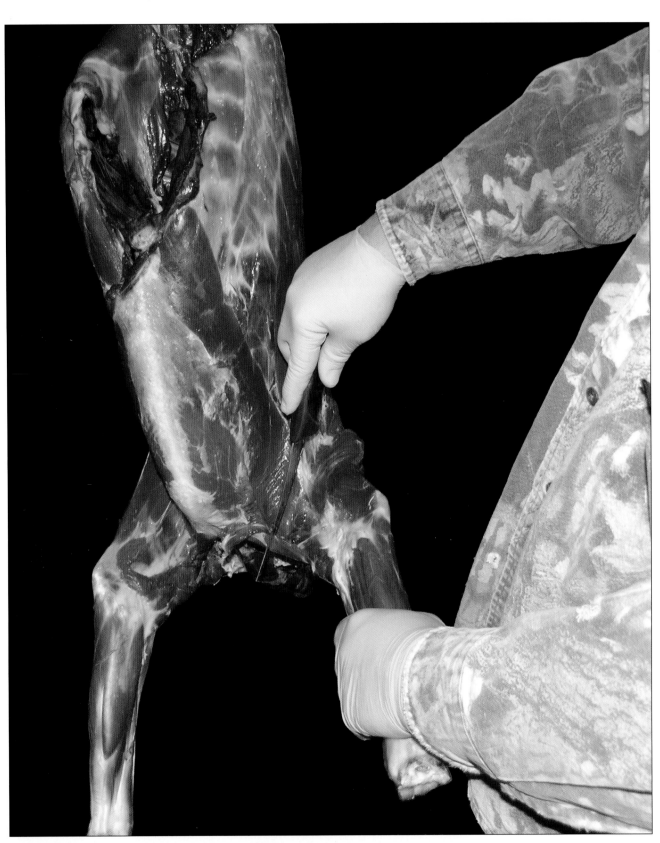

After skinning the deer, you'll continue with the rest of the butchering process.

"I've cleaned my own fish and birds, but..."

It's only natural to feel a little squeamish the first time you do this. And let's face it, the first time or two cutting up a deer will probably feel different from cutting up a fish or a pheasant. That's especially true if you're a new hunter or new to hunting larger game.

If you've made a good shot, your quarry's transition will be brief and humane. For you, the psychological transition may take a little longer. Just remember that your deer is no longer a live, animated animal. It's an inanimate object. It's protein. It's what's for dinner. Dozens of dinners, in fact, over the next several months.

When you field-dress a deer the process will involve some warm blood. You'll be working on a recently dead animal. You can remind yourself that it's no longer alive, but it's still going to feel like a dead animal.

Later, when you get your deer home, you'll remove its head and lower legs. That's a little harsh, but by then you'll be used to the idea that this is a very dead deer. It's a carcass that you're about to skin, butcher and turn into venison. A few minutes later, once your deer is headless, footless and up on the gambrel, it will definitely feel much more like venison.

After removing each piece from the carcass, you'll work on it more at a bench or table.

Some pieces will be destined for stew, burger or sausage. If you're grinding them up for hamburger or sausage, you may decide to save that step for later.

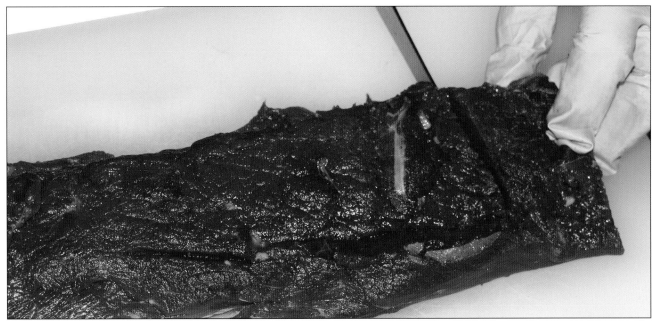

You'll cut some pieces into roasts and slice other pieces across the grain to make steaks. Then you'll wrap these pieces for the freezer.

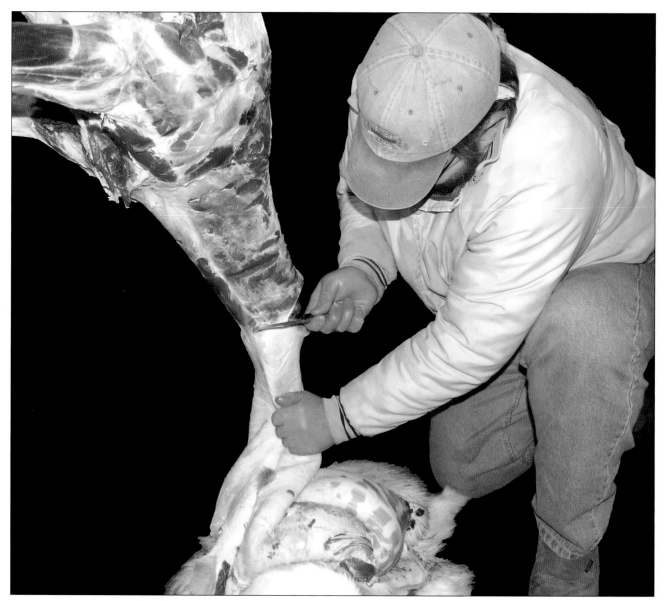

Once the hide is removed, it will feel less like a deer and more like venison.

As you begin the job of skinning, however, it may once again feel like you're working on a dead deer. After all, there's all that… deerskin. But once you've finished this step, especially if it's your very first deer, this will probably be the biggest transitional moment. From here on, it will feel less like you're cutting up a dead animal and more like you're cutting up venison.

Field-Dressing Your Deer

Field-dressing is the process of getting the insides out of your deer before getting your deer out of the woods. It's a dirty job, but someone's got to do it—probably you—even if you pay someone else to take it from there.

Even the very first time, this will probably only take ten or fifteen minutes. After you've done it a few more times it will only take you a couple of minutes.

Later we'll explain all the details. But if you're new to all this, here's what to expect.

You'll start by making some small, precise cuts in the pelvic area. After that, you'll slit

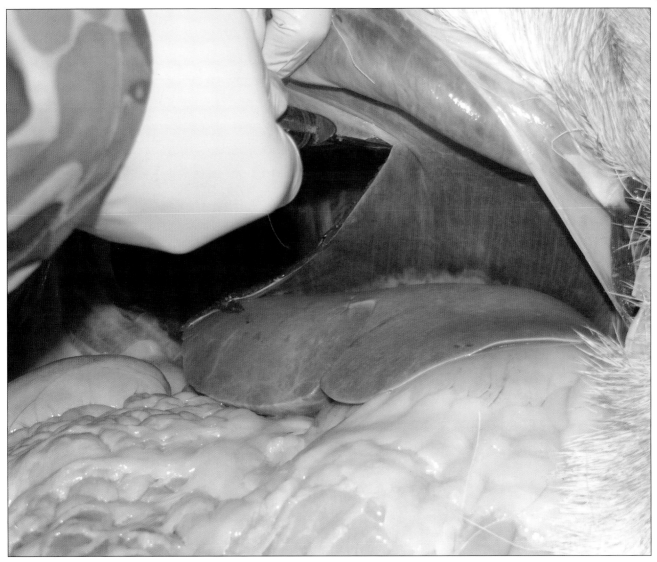

The diaphragm separates the lungs from the abdominal cavity.

the abdomen forward to the sternum. You may decide to saw through the pelvis and sternum; these steps are optional.

Next, you'll cut through the diaphragm. If you've made a good shot through the heart-lung area, there might be some blood in there. It will be pints rather than gallons; just be ready for it to come pouring out when you cut through the diaphragm.

You'll then reach in to cut the trachea and esophagus. Once you've done that, you'll be ready to pull everything out into a pile. Then you'll lift the deer by its front legs to pour out any remaining blood. From here on, it just gets easier.

Skinning Your Deer

The first time you do it, this part of the job can seem a little overwhelming. But if you use a sharp knife and take it step-by-step it's not bad.

Your goal is to remove the skin in one intact piece. At various moments you'll be cutting, peeling and pulling. On some parts of the deer you'll be cutting to free every square inch of

GET A GRIP

By the way, here are some tips than can reduce strain on your hands and wrists:

- *Use a rag or an old towel for better grip on the slippery inside of the hide. When you can grip the outside and the inside, you'll have more options.*

- *Pull with one hand while pushing with the other hand. While pulling downward with one hand, use your other to push the skin downward and outward.*

- *Use your elbow for better leverage. While pulling downward with one hand, use your other elbow to push the skin downward and outward.*

Use your elbow to push down the skin.

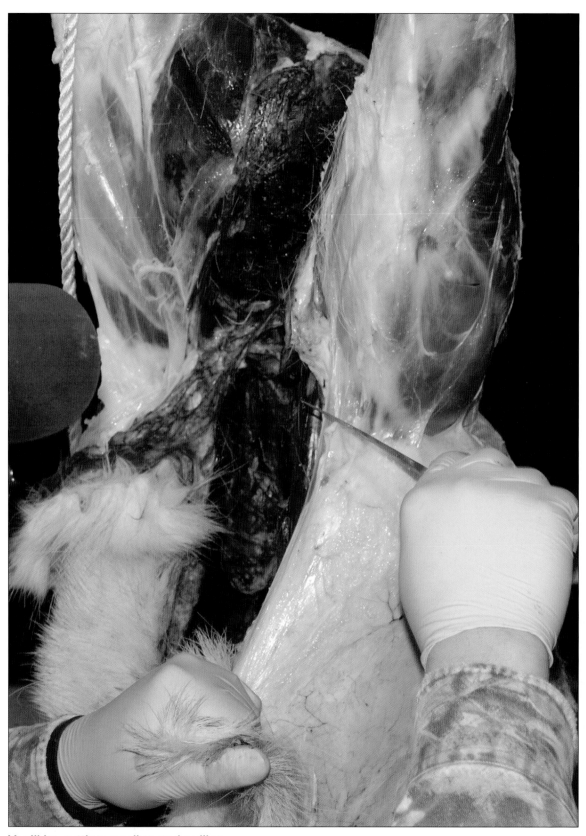

You'll be cutting, peeling and pulling.

skin. In other areas you'll be able to set down your knife and just pull the skin free. It's much easier to make progress that way. The general idea is to pull when you can and cut when you must.

Mostly you'll be pulling and cutting at the same time. While pulling on the hide, you'll slice away at the fat and connective tissue in the seam you're exposing between the hide and the meat. Rather than pressing hard with the knife you'll use a gentle sweeping motion. As you pull back the skin and expose a new "seam" you'll continue in a similar fashion.

Every deer is different; some are easier to skin than others. Younger deer are generally easier to skin. Freshly killed deer are also easier to skin. If you can skin a deer within the first day or two, the job will be much easier.

Keep in mind, too, that it's just about impossible to skin a frozen deer. You'll need to somehow thaw it first. This may take a while; deer hair is extremely good insulation.

Even on the same deer, some areas will be harder to skin than others. On the lower legs and the neck you'll need to cut every inch of the way. That's especially true for the neck of a rutting buck. On some parts of the deer, however, you'll be able to cut less and do a lot more pulling and peeling.

We'll show you a better, more modern method.

With this method, you'll quickly turn your deer into dozens of delicious dinners.

If a few scraps of meat are left on the hide, don't worry about it. And don't worry about a few cuts that go through the skin. You're probably not sending your deerskin to the taxidermist for a full body mount. Just think of those cuts as extra finger holes that you can use for pulling.

When you use these techniques and find the right balance of pulling, peeling and cutting, the job will go fast. You won't need mechanical claws, tongs or other gadgets. You'll do just fine with two hands, two elbows and one sharp knife.

Butchering Your Deer

With the method we're about to show you, you'll be able to quickly turn each deer into dozens of delicious dinners. The cuts of meat you end up with will look different from the roasts, chops and steaks you're used to seeing at the grocery store; they won't include any fat, gristle or bone. Instead of T-bones, for example, you'll be eating lean, luscious, boneless backstrap.

Better yet, you won't need to saw through bones and you won't be spraying sawdust and bone chips all over your venison. In fact, with the method we're about to show you the only tool you'll need is a sharp knife. Rather than cutting through bones you'll cut through the spaces between the bones.

You will still need to cut through tendons and connective tissues. With a sharp knife, however, you'll be able to slice right through them. If the edge of your knife hits bone, then you'll explore a little and try for a different angle.

You'll disassemble your deer one piece at a

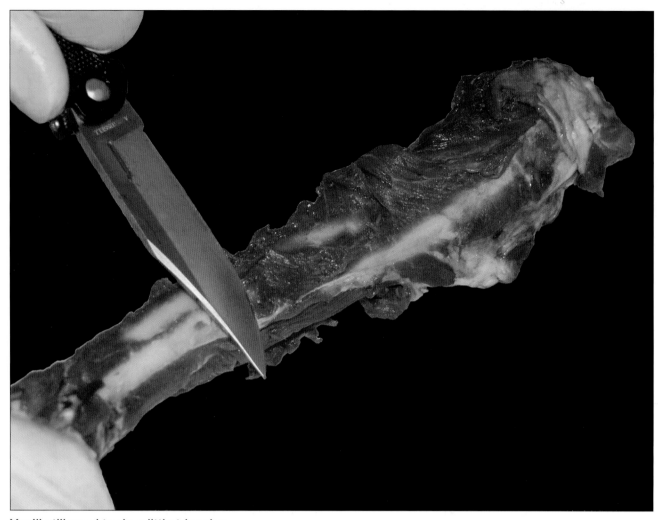

You'll still need to do a little trimming.

time. After you cut each piece free, you'll take it down and work on it more at a bench or table. Finally, when only the hindquarters are left hanging on the gambrel, you'll take down this last piece for further disassembly.

You'll begin with the front legs. Amazingly, they have no bone-to-bone connection at all; they're only attached by tendons and ligaments. This gives deer extra flexibility, which in turn makes for more speed and agility. By coincidence, it also makes for easier butchering. With practice and with a sharp knife you'll be able to remove each front leg with only a few strokes.

A deer's rear legs are attached with a ball-and-socket joint that's a little trickier to negotiate.

But once you find the right path it will only take a few slices. Then, when you sever the final tendon, you'll feel the joint almost fall apart.

You'll also sever the spine in two places—once just forward of the hindquarters, and once at the base of the tail when you're skinning your deer. In both cases, you'll carefully slice through the disks between the vertebrae.

At a bench or table, you'll cut up various large chunks. You'll use certain joints and bones as landmarks, but avoid cutting against the bone. Instead, slide your knife alongside the bones. Sometimes this is simple; other times it requires more careful maneuvering.

You'll trim away any fat from the outside of

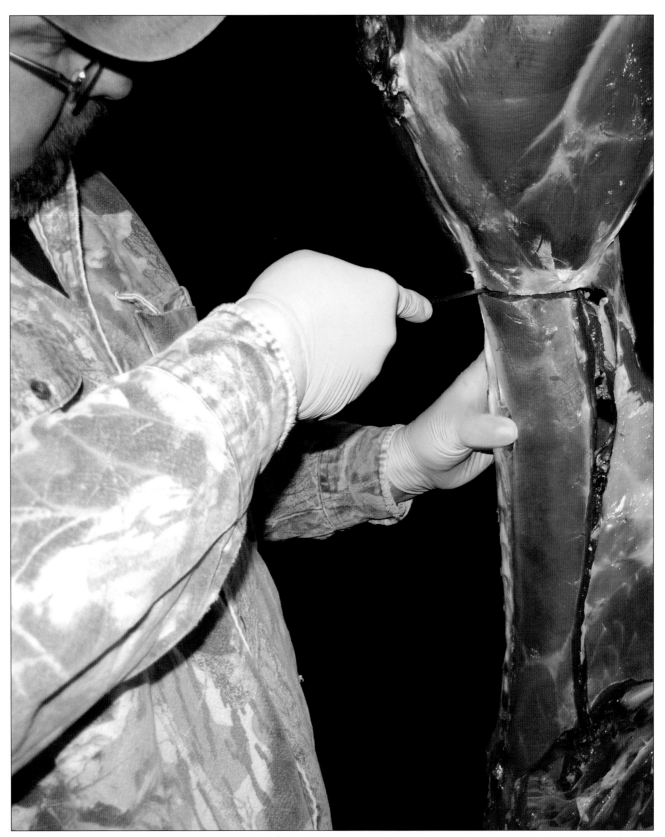

Some deer are much leaner than others.

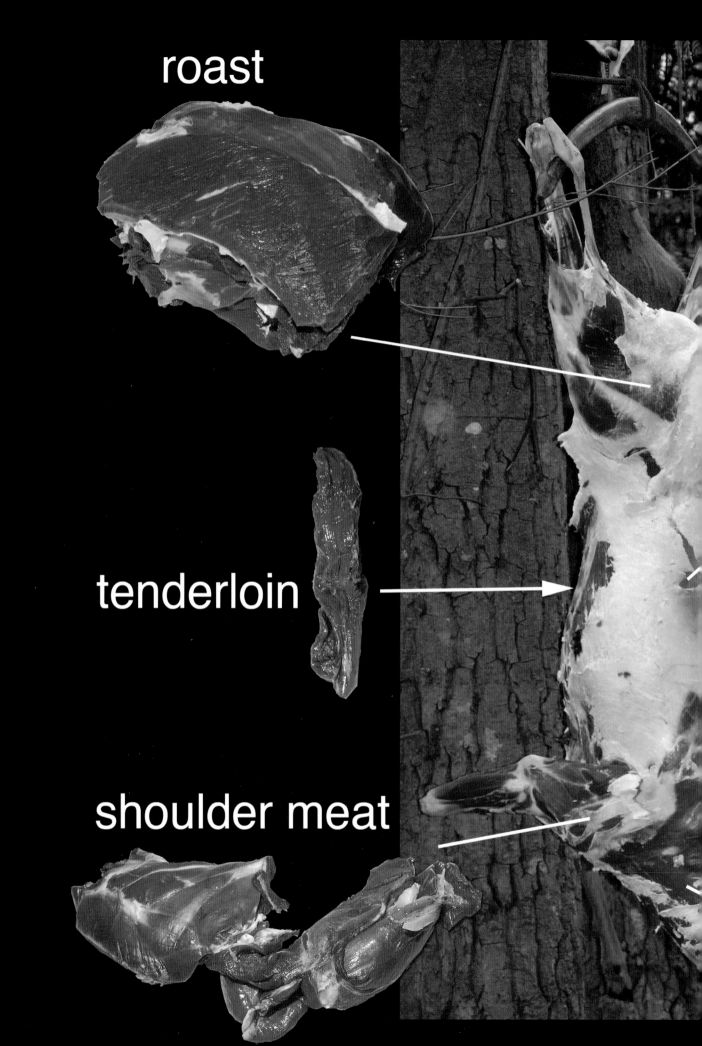

roast

tenderloin

shoulder meat

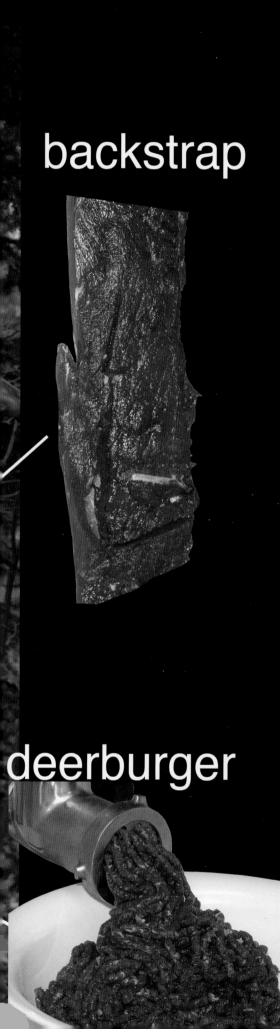

backstrap

deerburger

these larger pieces, then separate the meat from the bone and trim away any remaining fat, connective tissue and "silverskin." When done, you'll have many pieces of lean, boneless meat that don't include any chewy, gristly bits.

Some of these chunks will be large and tender; they'll make great roasts. Or by slicing across the grain of the muscle fibers you'll turn them into steaks. Other pieces will be smaller or from parts of the deer that tend to be a little tougher. You'll use these pieces for stew, hamburger or sausage.

As you'll see from the photos in this book, some deer are much leaner than others. Young deer that are still growing can be as lean as jackrabbits. Similarly, in late fall, a rutting buck is likely to be especially lean; its meat may have an almost bluish tinge. Other deer, however, have a thick layer of subcutaneous fat, plus more pockets of fat on the inside of the abdominal cavity and between various muscle groups.

But there's one place you'll never see much fat on a deer—marbled right into the meat, as it often is with beef. Most of the fat will be easy to trim away and you'll want to get as much as you can. A few pieces here and there, however, are nothing to worry about.

The Hundred-Cow Hamburger

Modern meatpacking plants are huge operations; every day, they accept cattle from hundreds of different sources. And every day, each plant churns out hundreds of tons of ground beef—sometimes even thousands of tons. Then they stuff it into 80-pound plastic tubes and ship it to grocery stores all over the country. There, it's often reground and mixed with the store's trimmings—or even with meat that's unsold after being out on the shelf for a few days.

Some organisms finding their way into this supply chain are especially virulent; it doesn't take many of them to cause illness in humans. Epidemiologists have calculated that a single animal infected with *E. Coli* 0157:H7 can contaminate up to eight tons of ground beef.* As Eric Schlosser writes in his book *Fast Food Nation*, "a single fast-food hamburger now contains meat from dozens or even hundreds of different cattle."

If you grind your own venison, on the other hand, most of your deerburgers will contain meat from only one deer. Or, if you and a few friends really gear up for some mass-produced deerburger, maybe two or three deer. What's more, you'll know exactly where that meat has been and how it's been handled at every step of the way.

Armstrong, et al. "Emerging Foodborne Pathogens: Escherichia coli O157:H7 as a Model of Entry of a New Pathogen in the Food Supply of the Developed World"

What's For Dinner

Here's a look at the finished products you'll end up with when you're done—and also where you'll obtain each cut.

How Many Dinners Per Deer?

By now you're probably wondering "Okay. How *many* dinners per deer?" Before we continue, it's time for a quick reality check.

Unfortunately, the average deer, whether whitetail or mule deer, isn't nearly as large as most hunters would like to believe. Even a buck that dresses out to 200 pounds is extremely unusual. Depending on where you hunt, it might be more realistic to plan on a deer that, after field-dressing, weighs somewhere between 75 and 125 pounds.

Next, we need to do a little more subtracting. You probably won't want to eat the head, feet, hide or bones. You're also going to trim off and discard nearly all of the fat. While deer are leaner than cattle or hogs, this could account for several more pounds.

The bottom line? On average, slightly less than half of a deer's field-dressed weight will be boneless, edible meat. If you've shot a deer that dresses out at 120 pounds, you'll end up with around 55 pounds of venison—maybe less if there's a lot of damage from your bullet.

Fortunately, however, it's all lean, delicious, boneless meat. You won't waste room in your freezer by packaging up bones and fat, and each package will go a long way.

In fact, here's something to keep in mind when you wrap your venison for the freezer; we'll mention it again when we get to that chapter. All of your venison will be lean, boneless meat that isn't going to shrink dramatically during cooking.

Because of that, most people will be satisfied with a significantly smaller portion than they'd prefer if they were eating beef or pork. But if you'd rather fill your freezer with fewer but larger packages, go for it. Just don't say we didn't warn you.

EVEN IF YOU COULD BUY IT IN THE STORE...

Here in the U.S., the federal Lacey Act of 1900 ended the era of market hunting for good. All commercially available venison is now raised on farms. As delicious as it may be, purists feel that it's not quite the nutritional and culinary equivalent of wild venison.

Still, it's entirely possible to pull out your credit card and have a package of frozen venison steaks express-delivered right to your door. The other day we did a little on-line comparison shopping. The best price we were able to find on boneless backstrap was about $42.50 per pound. By the time you read this, of course, prices may have gone up.

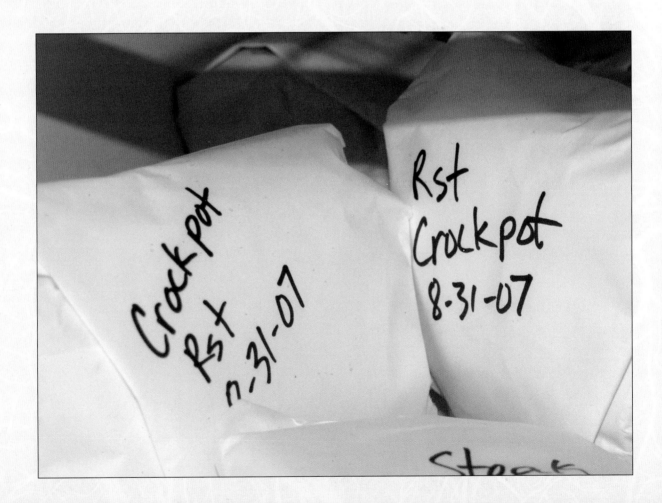

"I don't like venison, but that was delicious!"

Some day you may hear words like these from one of your dinner guests. Unfortunately people have a lot of biases about wild game; they expect it to taste, well, "gamey."

While venison naturally tastes different from beef, it doesn't naturally taste gamey. Venison is naturally delicious; that's why deer have learned to hide well and run fast.

We can't emphasize this enough. Venison tastes good. Bad venison doesn't start out that way. It goes bad somewhere along the way.

If beef were treated the way some people treat their venison, beef would taste pretty strange too. You rarely see rows of dead cattle hanging from a tree in "cattle camp" until they're hauled back to the city for butchering. And on warm, sunny November days, you'll almost never see caravans of dead black angus riding across the width of an entire state atop big, black SUVs.

Instead, most meat packers pack meat fast. Along the way they keep it clean and cool. Later, we'll tell you more about how to take care of your venison, but this should give you a darn good start.

Wild game doesn't naturally taste "gamey."

CHAPTER 2

Gearing Up and Getting Ready

Photo courtesy of Jacob Edson

Deer season is coming; let's gear up and get ready. In this chapter, we'll talk about the essentials you need now, the investments you can put off for a year or two, and the gadgets you'll never, ever need.

BEFORE YOU SHOOT

Before you shoot a deer, ask yourself a few questions:

· Do I really want to drag a deer through that swamp I just waded across?

· How am I going to get a deer out of the woods and back to my vehicle from here?

· How am I going to get a deer on or in my vehicle—especially if it's that big buck I've been tracking?

· Once I get a deer loaded up, how long will it take me to get home from here?

· When will I actually be able to do the butchering?

· How will I keep this deer cool enough until then?

· How will I keep this deer from freezing until then?

· By the way… How much room do I still have in my freezer?

· Do I have all the supplies I'll need for butchering and packaging my venison?

· If I need to get this deer disassembled fast, will I be able to cancel that sales meeting and take a day off work tomorrow?

· If it's going to be warm the next few days, and if we're waking up the kids early tomorrow morning so we can drive to Grandma's for Thanksgiving weekend, then should I even be going hunting tonight?

Ten or twenty feet of parachute cord will fit nicely in your pocket.

Getting Your Deer Out of the Woods

Maybe you've dropped your deer in the middle of a hayfield or right at the edge of a logging trail. You may be able to drive right up to it. That's not, however, something you can always count on. Instead, you may have a mile or so of thick brush between you and the nearest road.

Fortunately there are plenty of tricks that make the job easier, like wheeled carts, plastic sleds, straps and harnesses for dragging, and special ramps for when you get back to your vehicle.

Inexpensive plastic sleds work great when there's snow on the ground—and even when there isn't. Even on grass and leaves they pres-

ent less friction than deer fur. They also allow you to get your deer out of the woods in much better condition. Then, once you get back to your vehicle, they can double as a makeshift ramp.

Even if you have a cart or sled back at your vehicle, we recommend that you always carry a length of the strong, lightweight cord sold as "parachute cord." A piece ten or fifteen feet long only weighs an ounce or so.

Don't worry about this small-diameter cord cutting into your hands when you're dragging a heavy deer; we have a solution. Just break off a stick that's a couple feet long and an inch or so in diameter. That will be your handle. Tie one end of the cord around the center of the stick, and the other end around the deer's antlers or neck. Then grab the stick and start walking.

You can also buy various straps and harnesses designed to make dragging a deer even easier; most of them only cost a few dollars. But try them out before you actually need them. In the end, you may decide the old "string and stick" method works just fine.

Once back at your vehicle you'll want to lay out a tarp to catch any blood that drains out on the way home. Most of it will be drained out by now, but not all of it.

Even if you're driving a pickup with an open bed, a tarp's a good idea. We recommend one of the inexpensive blue ones that you can find at any hardware store; usually the smallest size is big enough. And, as much as we hate to waste this sort of thing, you'll probably want to use each tarp once and then throw it away. They're

The rafters are ready.

You'll need a gambrel for hanging your deer.

Rule #1: Bring a Knife

Until now, I haven't told many people this story. It's a little embarrassing. But one October afternoon, a long, long time ago…

I was in a hurry to get in a little bowhunting during that last hour before dark. I'd placed my stand a long way from the road, so I knew I'd better get going. I grabbed my gear and headed down the trail.

I made a good shot, a nice buck, and the deer went down right there. Fortunately, I wouldn't be following a blood trail in the dark. No need to go all the way back to the truck for a flashlight. There was still a little light left for field-dressing. Things were going great.

That was when I discovered that I didn't have a knife. I took a moment to consider my options. Maybe there was a knife somewhere in the truck. Did I still have that old jackknife in the bottom of the glove compartment?

But by the time I got to the truck and back, it would be dark. The deer would be tough to drag out if I didn't field-dress it. If there wasn't a knife in the truck, then I'd also have to lift the deer into the truck without field-dressing it.

My truck was parked at the end of a logging trail, several hundred yards from the road—a dirt road that might not see any other vehicles until tomorrow or the next day. I wasn't going to have any help. I could go all the way home for a knife and come back. But those coyote tracks I'd seen on the way out to my stand…

Then I noticed the arrows still in my quiver. Back then, most broadheads were simpler; I was using a two-bladed design that I knew was razor sharp. If I held the shaft of the arrow just right, and if I carefully avoided the other edge of the broadhead…

It worked. Not great, but better than you might think. Still, I've never forgotten my knife again. Not once. Plus, I always bring a small folding knife as a backup.

The moral of the story: There are several. First, always bring a knife. And maybe an extra knife. These days, you can buy a top-quality pocket knife that only weighs a few ounces. Some of them work well enough so you'd never need anything larger.

Second, while a broadhead may not be the perfect tool for the job, small and sharp always beats big and dull. And third, you don't necessarily need to cut through the sternum and pelvis when you're field-dressing a deer. In some cases, it's better if you don't. We'll tell you more about that later, when we get to that chapter on field-dressing.

not totally impermeable and they're difficult to get completely clean.

Next, you'll need to get your deer on or in your vehicle. Sometimes that can be a real challenge—especially if you're out in the woods by yourself and shot a large, heavy buck. You may want to bring a few boards for a ramp, and maybe extra rope to help with the hoisting and pulling.

When *You* Get Out of the Woods

Maybe you downed your deer a few hundred yards from your vehicle, and maybe you're only a few miles from home. Maybe it's warm and sunny and maybe you'll be back in time for lunch. Or maybe not.

Chances are just as good that it's now dark, cold, and raining or snowing. You've been up since 4:00 a.m. You field-dressed your deer and dragged it for a half-mile through the woods. You're exhausted, hungry, thirsty and soaked with some combination of sweat, sleet and deer blood.

You finally reach your vehicle. When you get there let's hope you find spare clothes, a snack and something to drink. Even if you're not covered in mud and blood, a fresh change of clothes can make for a more comfortable ride home.

Hoists, Gambrels and Game Bags

When you get home you'll need to get your deer hung up—first to get it off the ground, and later so you'll be able to work on it comfortably when skinning and butchering it.

From Left to right: Eric's old favorite, a lightweight 4¼-inch blade that's been used to field-dress dozens of deer. A heavy folder with a 3¾-inch blade. A light folder with a 3-inch blade. A typical scalpel. Not shown: A classic Bowie knife with a 10-inch blade. If we had one, we would have only bought it for this picture.

Save your back. An inexpensive hoist is well worth the money. You'll find a variety of options for sale at just about any outdoor store. Some come with built-in locking mechanisms; others may lack this feature.

Either way, we suggest an additional cleat or tie-off system for extra safety. I bought a few from the boating department at my local hardware store and then just screwed them to the rafters in my garage. Eric has a similar system in his garage.

And speaking of the boating department... Many hunters in our area have bolted hand-crank boat-trailer winches to the wall of their garage. Strategically position a few pulleys and you can lift your deer into position with a few turns of the crank.

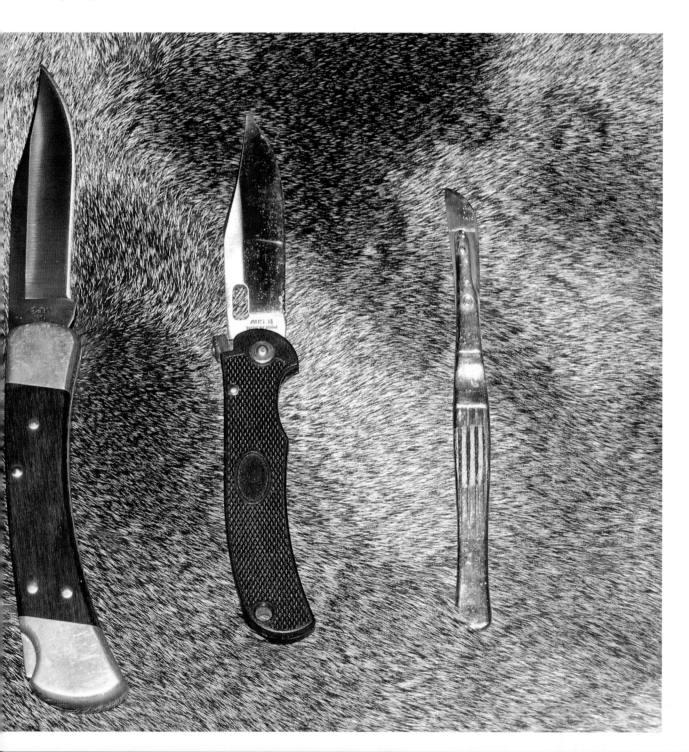

If you're concerned about CWD, you may decide to not use your kitchen knives for butchering. You may also want to designate a separate knife that you'll use for two steps that require severing the spinal cord. Don't use that knife for anything else.

At larger outdoor stores you'll even see electric hoists; they're smaller versions of the hoists you might see out on a factory floor. These only cost a few dollars more than a good pulley system and may even be easier to install.

To hang your deer for butchering, you'll also need a gambrel; you can find these at most large outdoor stores. They come in a variety of sizes and weight ratings. If you're hunting for deer, you won't need one rated for 1000-pound elk.

Instead, if you're feeling optimistic, buy two or three lighter-duty gambrels.

If your deer will hang for even a few hours in warm weather, you may want to consider a cheesecloth game bag. It keeps insects off the carcass and may also prevent the meat from drying out as rapidly.

Finally, have a few sheets of cardboard ready to put down on the floor. They'll absorb any remaining blood that drips out. You'll probably be able to pull them aside and discard them when you begin butchering; at that point the deer will be pretty well drained.

A Sharp Knife: Your Most Important Tool

A sharp knife is your most important tool. That's true when you're field-dressing your deer and it's true when you're back home butchering it. In fact, with the method we'll show you in this book, it's almost the only tool you'll need. You won't need meat saws, hatchets or giant cleavers. You'll need a good hunting knife plus a few knives to use for butchering. But before you go shopping, check your kitchen and your tackle box. You may already have everything you need. And when you head out into the woods, we suggest you skip the giant bowie knife with the ten-inch blade.

This Sagen Saw is the right tool for the job.

Hunting Knives:
Why Bigger Isn't Better

We recommend using knives with a blade between two and a half inches and four inches long. A smaller blade will give you much more control and precision; that's one reason surgeons use scalpels rather than bowie knives.

Using a larger blade only increases the chance that you'll cut something you don't want to cut. Potentially, that includes your own fingers. A larger blade is also much more difficult to maneuver when you're reaching way inside the deer during certain field-dressing steps; more about that later.

Specialized tools like this Wyoming Knife are worth a try.

Plus, when you're not using your knife you'll be carrying it. A small folding knife fits in your pocket and a larger one can ride in a belt sheath. Even if you prefer fixed-blade knives, a shorter knife is lighter and less likely to catch on the brush or get in the way when you sit down.

Good steel matters; pretty handles don't. Invest in a quality knife and learn how to keep it sharp. When you consider the money you spent on all your other hunting gear, it doesn't make sense to rely on a cheap knife—or far worse, an expensive dull knife.

Guthooks, Gadgets and Gimmicks

Today there are probably more hunting knives being sold with guthooks than without them. In theory this feature makes it easier for you to slit the abdominal wall and perform certain other field-dressing cuts. It's also meant to reduce the risk that you'll accidentally puncture internal organs during these steps.

In practice, however, the steps during which a guthook would be helpful are relatively easy. You'll spend more of your time on steps during which a guthook would get in the way and actually make the job harder. Plus, guthooks can be awkward to sharpen, and some designs are easily clogged with hair or bits of skin.

If you'd like to experiment with the whole concept, try one of the inexpensive tools made just for this purpose. Most come with replaceable blades that don't require sharpening. Bring one of these and your knife, and you'll be set.

There's one small tool that we recommend very highly. It's available from a couple of man-

You may already have most of the knives you need.

CHRONIC WASTING DISEASE (CWD): THE THREAT IS REAL

In recent years, you've probably begun hearing about Chronic Wasting Disease (CWD). It's a fatal neurological disease that affects ungulates like deer, elk and moose. So far, there's no conclusive evidence that it can infect humans. Neither, on the other hand, is there conclusive evidence that it can't. What's more, we know that certain diseases closely related to CWD definitely *can* be transmitted to humans from other species.

Since CWD is likely to work the same way as these other diseases, someone would probably begin experiencing their first symptoms after being infected for at least two or three years, and possibly as long as ten or fifteen years. They'd still hang on for several months after the first symptoms appeared; they'd only be *wishing* they were dead.

Even if you hunt in an area where deer are known to be infected with CWD, the risks may be extremely low. Still, the consequences are extremely high.

Until recently, some "experts" were writing in hunting magazines that CWD posed absolutely zero risk to humans—and not even all that much risk to deer. They wrote that anyone who claimed otherwise was a hysterical alarmist bent on exaggerating and sensationalizing the dangers. Unfortunately, these writers were not scientists. They didn't fully understand the disease, its causes or its epidemiology. See page 44 to learn more about this issue.

ufacturers; it's variously known as a "sternum saw" or a "pelvic saw."

These small T-handled saws are specially designed for cutting through the pelvis and sternum without puncturing any adjacent organs. The blade is short, it's designed to cut on the upward "pull" stroke, and it has a little "bumper" on the end so it won't puncture the bladder, intestine or any other internal organs. It's the right tool for the job.

A sturdy hunting knife can work for cutting the sternum and pelvis, but it's not great—especially when you get to the pelvis. For an older and larger deer, you may need to hold your knife with one hand while you hammer the butt of the knife with your other hand. This traditional technique is a good way to injure or cut yourself. At the very least you can count on bruising the heel of your hand. And because the next steps require a little prying and levering, there's always the chance that you could break the tip off your knife. Over the years I've done this several times.

Instead, we recommend that you spend around $15 on one of these specialized tools. For the average hunter, it will last a lifetime.

In outdoor shops and catalogs you'll see saws, claws and dozens of other gadgets and gimmicks that promise to speed or simplify the whole process of field-dressing, skinning and butchering. Save your money.

Instead, use it to buy a copy of this book, a good knife and the tools you really need. If you still feel like splurging, buy an extra dozen arrows or a few more boxes of ammunition. Then go get in some practice.

Grinding up a winter's supply of deerburger.

CHRONIC WASTING DISEASE (CWD): WHAT YOU CAN DO

So far, there are only a few small areas in North America where deer are known to be infected with CWD. But if you live in one of these areas, CWD is something you should take seriously. It's not a reason to stop hunting deer, and it's not a reason to stop eating venison. It is, however, a reason to start taking a few common-sense precautions.

What is CWD?

The family of diseases to which CWD belongs is called transmissible spongiform encephalopathies (TSEs). In plain language, that means contagious diseases that turn your brain into a sponge.

The best-known of these diseases is Bovine Spongiform Encephalopathy (BSE); it's more commonly known as mad cow disease. Scrapie is another TSE that infects sheep, but can't be transmitted to humans. Historically, the only TSE infecting humans in the developed world has been Creutzfeld-Jacob Disease (CJD); every year, it affects about one out of every million people—usually the elderly.

Then, in the 80s and 90s, a new variation surfaced in Britain. Initially, in fact, it was labeled "new variant CJD." It produced slightly different symptoms, and it often affected people who were much younger. It turned out that all of them had contracted the disease by eating beef containing nervous system tissues infected with BSE.

Of all the millions of Britons eating beef during that period, only about 150 had contracted the disease. To them, however, that was little comfort. In humans, the symptoms include convulsions, balance and coordination problems, dementia, and death. There is no cure, and the disease is always fatal.

Mad cow disease, CWD, and other TSEs aren't caused by a bacteria, or even by a virus. They're caused by something called a prion (pronounced "pree-on"). That's short for "proteinaceous infectious agent." It's a single molecule of protein that folds in an abnormal, unnatural fashion. When it gets close to a normal protein, it makes the other protein fold abnormally, too. Soon, there's a cascading chain reaction all over the nervous system.

Because the protein is folded in an unnatural way, the host's naturally occurring enzymes can't recognize and destroy it as they would other foreign proteins. It's also difficult to destroy prions with ultraviolet light, freezing or cooking. An autoclave used to disinfect surgical instruments has little effect on CWD prions. In the soil, they may be able to remain infectious for decades.

Extreme heat can destroy prions, as can certain chemicals. You'll notice that we've used the word "destroy" rather than "kill." That's because technically, prions aren't exactly alive.

Labs that perform CWD testing or research often employ a giant "deer digester." Like a pressure cooker on steroids, these tissue digesters rely on heat, pressure and caustic chemicals to create a sterile slurry that can safely be disposed of in a sanitary sewer.

The most effective measure available to the average person is probably to give knives and other equipment a prolonged soak in a 50/50 solution of water and chlorine bleach. An even stronger bleach solution might not be a bad idea.

Weighing the Risks

Science tells us that the risks may be low, but the consequences are high. Different people may weigh this sort of risk differently. Us? We tend to think about CWD precautions the same way we'd think about seat belts, fire extinguishers or smoke alarms. If it's no extra time or hassle, then why not play it safe?

So far, there are no documented cases of CWD being transmitted to humans. There are, in fact, other precedents for TSEs that don't seem able to jump the species barrier in the same way BSE can; one example is scrapie in sheep. Still, there are no guarantees.

The first precaution, of course, would be to not shoot and eat a deer that's obviously sick or acting strangely. A deer or elk infected with CWD would eventually exhibit extreme weight loss and a range of neurological symptoms that include an altered gait, weakness, strange behaviors and a decreased fear of people. If you see a deer like that, you probably wouldn't want to shoot and eat it anyway.

(If you live or hunt in an area where deer are known to be infected with CWD, check your local game laws to find out what you should do if you spot a deer with suspicious symptoms. In most locales, hunters are asked to not shoot these deer, but to contact their local conservation officer with information about the deer's symptoms and where it was last seen.)

When deer are more recently infected, however, they may look perfectly normal—even though the disease has already begun spreading throughout their nervous system. And in just the past few years, researchers have been able to isolate a small number of prions from the muscle tissue of infected animals. It remains true, however, that prions are far more plentiful in the brain, the central nervous system, the spleen, the lymph glands, and the bones.

If you live or hunt in an area where CWD is known to be present, you'll want to especially avoid these particular parts of the deer. Don't eat them, and don't cut into them any more than necessary. If you do cut into them, even just to sever the spinal cord, you may want to use a separate knife designated just for this purpose. When you're done, soak the knife in a strong bleach solution.

Even if you *don't* live or hunt in an area where deer are known to be infected, you may still want to take a few simple precautions—like using a separate knife for steps that involve cutting through the spinal cord. (By doing so, you'll also avoid dulling the edge of your "good" knives during these steps.)

Finally, keep these risks in perspective. In all of North America, CWD is only known to be present in a few small areas. Even if that's where you live and hunt, you can minimize the risk by taking a few common-sense precautions.

Eating venison that's been handled correctly is at least as safe as eating meat from the grocery store; some would argue that it's much safer. Every day, we take much bigger risks without ever giving it a thought. While these risks may be less dramatic, they're just as real. Be careful out there.

On the way to and from your hunting spot, drive carefully and wear your seatbelt. If you're tired on the way home, stop for some coffee so you'll stay awake. But skip the cigarettes, and maybe even the glazed doughnuts. If the sun is going down, or if it's already dark out, drive even more carefully the rest of the way home. Watch out for deer.

Take These Common-Sense Precautions

Here's a quick list of some common-sense precautions you may want to take—especially if you live in an area where deer are known to be infected with CWD. It's adapted from a pamphlet available from the Wisconsin Department of Agriculture.

General Precautions:

· Don't eat the eyes, brain, spinal cord, spleen, tonsils or lymph nodes.

· Don't eat any part of a deer that appears sick.

· If your deer is sampled for CWD testing, wait for the test results before eating any of the venison.

During Field-Dressing:

· Wear rubber or latex gloves.

· Minimize contact with the brain, spinal cord, spleen or lymph nodes.

· Don't use household knives or utensils.

· Remove all internal organs.

· Clean knives and equipment of all residue. Disinfect with a 50/50 solution of chlorine bleach and water. Soak knives for at least an hour.

During Processing:

- Wear rubber or latex gloves.
- Minimize handling of brain or spinal tissues. If removing antlers, use a saw designated for that purpose only, and dispose of the blade.
- Don't cut through the spinal column except to remove the head. Use a knife designated only for this purpose.
- Bone out the meat from the deer and remove all fat and connective tissue. This will also remove lymph nodes.
- Dispose of hide, brain and spinal cord, eyes, spleen, tonsils, bones and head in a landfill or by other means available in your area.
- Thoroughly clean and sanitize equipment and work areas with bleach water after processing. Wipe down counters with a 50/50 solution and let dry.
- If processing deer from an area where CWD is known to be present, keep meat and trimmings from each deer separate.

We can't guarantee that following the steps in this book will keep you safe from CWD. But it's a good start. We've already told you about how this modern, boneless method is less work, saves freezer space and yields tastier venison. In terms of CWD risk, it also happens to be the *safest*.

Traditional butchering techniques, on the other hand, can dramatically *increase* the chances of transmitting CWD to humans. Whatever you may or may not believe about those odds, you'll be increasing them dramatically if you saw through lots of bones—especially if you decide to laboriously saw through the entire length of the deer's spinal column. As you make that cut, your saw will be showering bits of spinal cord all over your entire winter's supply of venison.

The Knives You'll Need Back Home

Back home you'll need knives for skinning and butchering. We suggest buying two or three knives with relatively thin, flexible blades around five inches long. You'll also want a few shorter knives for more precise trimming work.

For skinning, you'll want a blade with a little curve to it. Specialized skinning knives, however, are much larger and swept back in a more radical curve; that's not something you'll really need for skinning deer. Your hunting knife or one of your butcher knives will work just fine.

For now you may be able to get by with the knives you already own. With your hunting knife, a fillet knife, and a few paring knives and butcher knives from the kitchen, you may already have everything you need.

Keep Your Knives Sharp

When skinning and butchering a deer a sharp knife is your most important tool. Apart from the $15 pelvic saw mentioned a few pages back, it's pretty much the only tool you'll need. But that means dull knives just won't cut it.

Although a discussion of sharpening techniques is beyond the scope of this book, we can't emphasize enough the importance of keeping your knives sharp. Dull knives make deer disassembly difficult. Plus, dull knives are more dangerous. Keep them sharp.

Meat Grinders, Vacuum-Packing Systems and Other Accessories for a Home Butcher Shop

Sooner or later, you'll probably want to invest in a quality meat grinder. Skip the hand-cranked grinders and light-duty models that would be perfect if you're grinding two pounds of walnuts for a big batch of cookies. You'll want something more substantial when grinding 50 or 100 pounds of venison.

For a top-quality commercial-grade grinder you'll probably need to spend two or three hundred dollars. But, unless you're grinding venison from more than three or four deer per year, you probably won't need to spend more still on a larger, more powerful model. Consider this a lifetime investment, one you'll never regret.

Photo courtesy of SharpByCoop.coma

Vacuum packing systems are a great way to prevent freezer burn and preserve the flavor of frozen venison. We suggest, however, that you invest in a good grinder first. If the vacuum packing system has to wait until next year or the year after that, it's okay.

With the "paper and plastic" method we'll shown you later, your venison will keep in the freezer just fine for a year or more, with no freezer burn and no loss of flavor. But without a grinder, you'll be using your trimmings and tougher cuts in stew. You might eventually decide that you still really enjoy stew—just not quite so often.

Similarly, if your budget is tight, then gadgets like sausage-making nozzles, meat mixers, patty makers and jerky squirters are all fun accessories for later—maybe a lot later.

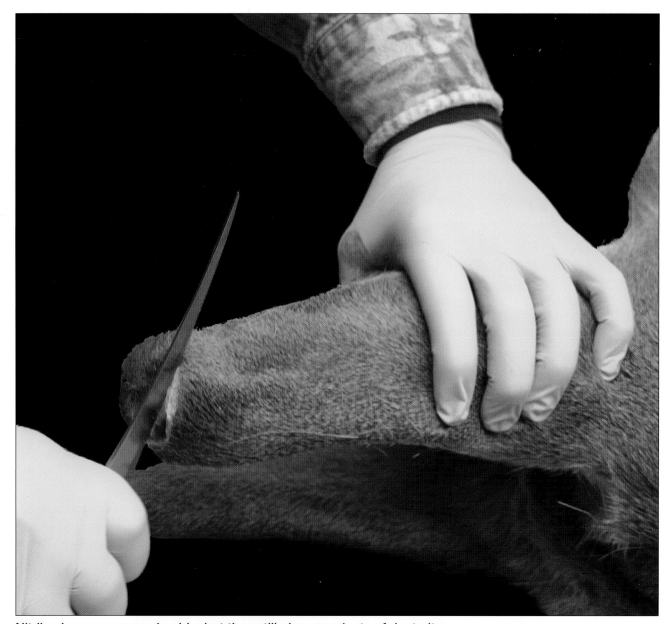

Nitrile gloves are more durable, but they still give you plenty of dexterity.

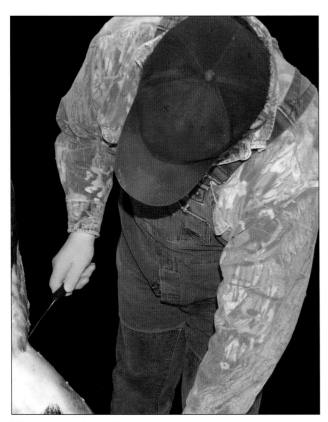

Dress For Success

Details make a difference. Let's take a quick look at the gloves, clothes and shoes that you'll want to wear in your home butcher shop.

Gloves

We recommend gloves made from a material called nitrile. Compared with latex or vinyl gloves, they offer better fit, comfort and durability. They also come in lovely colors, like the blues, greens and purples seen in most of this book's photos.

Clothes

In warm weather, just wear your oldest jeans and your oldest T-shirt or flannel. But in cold weather, how you dress becomes more important. If you're chilled to the bone for the next three hours, you won't just be uncomfortable. You'll also be stiffer and less coordinated, which increases the likelihood of accidents.

So if you're heading outdoors or to a poorly heated garage, make sure you're dressed warm-ly enough. Choose a warm jacket that you don't mind getting bloody. If you don't have anything you want to sacrifice, buy an inexpensive jacket or heavy sweatshirt that you'll reserve just for this purpose. From now on it'll be your butchering jacket.

Shoes

You'll probably be standing on concrete for at least a few hours. Your legs will ache less tomorrow if you wear shoes with supportive, cushioned soles.

Be warm, be comfortable, and wear something you don't mind spattering with a few drops of blood. If you're heading to the gym tomorrow night, then tonight you may not want to wear your favorite white cross-trainers.

Preparing Your Work Area

Next, what about that butcher shop you're about to open in the garage?

Even if you have a workbench in your garage, you may want to drag in that extra table from the patio. If neither are clean enough to pass an official USDA inspection, don't worry. In a moment you'll cover everything with white freezer paper. That keeps things cleaner during butchering and makes clean-up a lot easier when you're done.

Hold it down with a few pieces of masking tape or freezer tape. Until you're done butchering, you may want to borrow a tape dispenser from your home office.

Also round up a few extra cutting boards. Avoid glass or hard plastic that can damage knives. So you'll have plenty of room to work, stock up on inexpensive cutting boards made from thin plastic sheets.

Next, you'll need a few rags, plenty of paper towels and a bowl of warm water. You'll need pretty much every large bowl you have in your kitchen. Eventually, you may even want to invest in a few rectangular plastic meat tubs. For now, however, your favorite old popcorn bowls will do just fine.

And speaking of tubs...Designate a garbage can or an old washtub for leftover bones and scraps. Once a washtub has been used for this purpose, you probably won't want to use it again for icing beverages at your summer picnics. (Note to neighbors: We didn't.)

If it's going to be cold out and you'll be working in an unheated detached garage, you may want to invest in an indoor-rated propane heater. But plan ahead; if it's really cold out, your garage will need a few hours to warm up.

There. That just about takes care of it. You're pretty well geared up and ready to head for the woods. Let's go find some deer.

Not sure you can remember all those details? Check out the checklist on the next page.

Freezer paper is cheap. Use plenty.

Your "Gutting and Cutting" Checklist

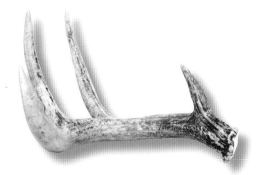

Make sure you have the following items…

1) With you at all times when you're hunting:

_ Knife.

_ Spare knife, just in case.

_ Gloves for field-dressing.

_ Pelvic saw or similar device (optional, but highly recommended).

_ A foot or two of light-duty cord for tying off the anal tract (optional).

_ Ten or fifteen feet of parachute cord for dragging your deer out of the woods.

_ Small steel or sharpening stone (optional).

_ Cheesecloth game bag (optional).

_ Paper towels for the deer and sanitary hand wipes for you (optional).

_ A plastic bag if you'd like to remove and save the heart, liver or tenderloins.

_ A small flashlight or headlamp if there's any chance you'll be out after dark.

_ Rifle, ammo, compass, lunch and all that other stuff you already knew about.

2) Back at your vehicle, just in case:

_ Flashlight and headlamp.

_ Game cart or plastic sled.

_ Paper towels and instant hand cleaning gel.

_ A snack and something to drink.

_ Extra warm clothes or rain gear. Or, depending on the weather, both.

_ An additional change of clothes reserved solely for the trip home.

_ A tarp, heavy rope and maybe a few boards to use as a loading ramp.

3) Waiting back home, so you'll be ready to open your own butcher shop:

_ Knives, already sharpened.

_ Hoist and gambrel.

_ Cardboard sheets for the floor.

_ Freezer tape, markers and multiple boxes of plastic wrap and freezer paper.

_ Rags, paper towels and a bucket of warm water.

_ Cutting boards and bowls or tubs for your venison.

_ A designated garbage can or washtub for leftover bones and scraps.

_ An indoor-rated garage heater if it's cold.

CHAPTER 3

Shop Before You Shoot, Aim Carefully, and Don't Shoot Your Steaks

Photo courtesy of Dan Schmidt

This is going to be a short chapter; there are already plenty of books out there about deer hunting. This book is mainly about what to do after you get one. Still, we'd like to say a few words about what happens just before that moment.

Surprisingly, this recipe was not a hit at deer camp.

Favorite Recipes for Antler Soup and Stir-Fried Antlers

If you're sitting out in the woods on the first morning of deer season and a stringy old buck with gigantic antlers strolls along and stands broadside forty feet in front of you, go ahead and take the shot. But remember that steaks and roasts from a doe or yearling buck will be more tender, they'll taste even better, and you'll still have plenty of hamburger or stew meat.

You've probably heard the old saying about how "you can't eat horns." After careful research and experimentation, we have to agree.

In the last chapter of this book, we will tell you more about how to save antlers—and even how to prepare your deer for the taxidermist if you'd like it mounted. But we've saved that chapter for last, right after we share a few tips on how to cook your venison. First things first.

The Best Aiming Points

You've probably already read this in a hundred hunting magazines, but it's still true: Bullet placement is the single most important predictor of stopping power.

It's also the single most important predictor of how much meat will be damaged. Sure, there are other variables. An arrow does less damage than a bullet, and some calibers cause less damage than others. All else equal, a .243 or a .30-30 will damage less meat than a .300 Winchester Magnum.

But with a well-placed shot, all of these calibers will put a deer down fast and none of them will damage much meat. Fortunately, the most humane shots are also the ones that waste the least meat.

Here's a quick review of the best aiming points. And if we may be a tiny bit dogmatic for a moment... Don't take any shot that's not pictured on the next few pages. In fact, here are

CHOOSING AMMUNITION

If you're a bowhunter, you don't need to worry about which caliber to choose. No arrow will damage as much meat as a bullet would; as the saying goes, you'll be able to "eat right up to the arrow hole." And if you're a bowhunter, you're probably already being pretty particular about where you aim. Your goal, after all, is a humane kill and a short blood trail.

Choosing a Cartridge for Deer

Your choice of a deer cartridge is a highly personal matter; most hunters already have their favorites. Some arrive at these choices after much thought, analysis, and experimentation. Others get there by default; they shoot what Dad or Grand-dad shot.

Since you probably already have a favorite deer cartridge of your own, we won't spend much time trying to change your mind. But maybe you're a new hunter. Or maybe you're an experienced hunter shopping for your next rifle. If so, here are a few things to consider as you ponder that choice.

Photo courtesy of Jacob Edson

Is More Better?

We'd say... Sometimes.

Bullet placement is everything. And no matter how much shooting you've done, you'll be able to shoot more accurately with a milder cartridge that produces less muzzle blast and recoil. Few benchrest matches are won with elephant rifles.

What's more, deer are not as big as elephants, or even elk. Very few deerhunting situations call for a magnum caliber.

One of them might be when you're hunting in terrain where you can reasonably expect some extra-long shots. With certain flatter-shooting magnum cartridges, you may be able to make an ethical shot at slightly longer ranges. For most deer hunters, however, accuracy is the limiting factor long before a flat trajectory or long-range stopping power would be.

Keep in mind, too, that over 90% of whitetail deer are shot at distances of less than 100 yards. (The average shot for mule deer might be slightly longer, but not by all that much.) That's not because of how far we can shoot. It's because of where the deer are; you're most likely to find them in the woods or on the edge of the woods.

Deer feel safer when they're in or near protective cover. Sure, you'll sometimes find tracks out in the middle of a wide-open hayfield. But those tracks were most likely made at night; the deer probably won't still be standing in them when the sun comes up.

It bears repeating; over 90% of whitetail deer are shot at distances of less than 100 yards. Nearly all of the other 10% are shot within distances of 200 yards; with recent advances in cartridge technology, that's within the effective range of a .30-30. Most standard non-magnum rifle cartridges are going to be effective on deer out to 300 yards and beyond. Still, for those overconfident deer that assume they're perfectly safe prancing around on the far side of that bean field...

Photo courtesy of www.greatoutdoorstudios.com

The other situation that may call for a magnum caliber? If you'll be using the same rifle for deer as you do for elk, caribou, and moose, then you'll need a cartridge that's up to the job. Practice enough so you can handle the recoil comfortably. Then aim carefully, just as you would if you were out there with a "milder" cartridge.

Hunters in those two situations may benefit from a magnum caliber. Most of us, however, will do just fine with something more moderate.

Too often, hunters get excited about the latest and greatest; they want the most powerful, flat-shooting cartridge they can find. And after all, gun writers need something new to write about in all those hunting magazines every month. Meanwhile, year after year, plenty of deer have been killed with old, standard cartridges that don't even have the word "magnum" in their name.

With proper bullet placement, and within its intended range, nearly any standard centerfire rifle caliber from a .243 on up will stop a deer in its tracks. (The few exceptions are anemic cartridges like the .30 carbine, which packs less punch than many "smaller" calibers.) But without proper bullet placement, even a much more potent cartridge won't result in a humane kill. It could, however, damage a lot more meat.

Together, the .30-30 and the .30-06 have probably accounted for more deer than all of the others put together. Both cartridges have been around for over a century. The .270 has been around since 1925, and even the .243 has been around since 1955. There's not much new to write about these four calibers this month. But they're still the four most popular, and they still keep killing deer.

What if you hunt in a slug-only area? Modern saboted slugs turn a 20 gauge into an adequate deer gun at moderate ranges. Because of its reduced recoil, many hunters will be able to shoot it more accurately than a 12. For both gauges, reduced-recoil loads may allow you to shoot more accurately and still have plenty of power to get the job done. One way or another, a good slug gun with a rifled barrel is plenty accurate out to 100 yards and beyond.

With saboted bullets, modern in-line muzzleloaders can match or exceed the ballistics achieved by shotgun slugs; the best are more accurate than many cartridge firearms. If you do your part, they'll do theirs.

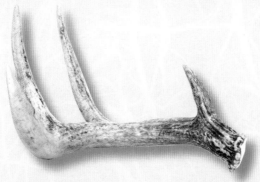

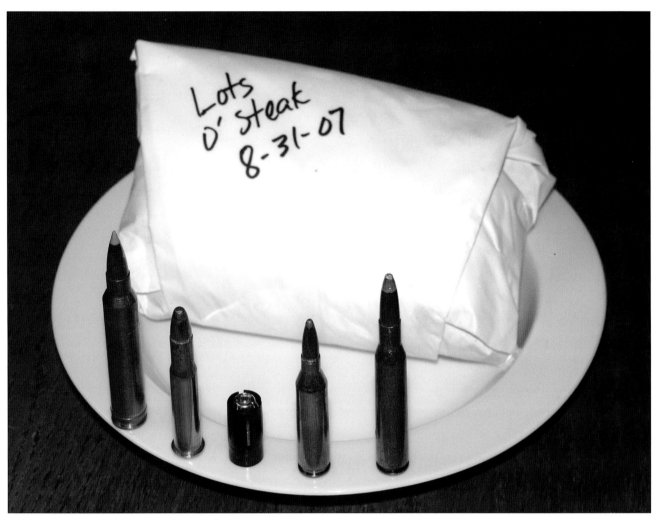

Most deer will never know the difference.

two shots that we suggest you never take—plus two more that are questionable:

- **Never shoot at the south end of a north-bound deer.** It's a view we've all seen—usually of a deer that saw us first. Don't give in to temptation.

- **Never aim for a deer's head.** Deer are constantly moving their heads around when you least expect it, and their brain is a fairly small target. Hunters who aim for a deer's head are just as likely to shoot off its nose or its lower jaw. When they do, the deer will die a slow, lingering death.

- **Think twice before trying a neck shot.** If you miss the spine, a neck-shot deer could travel a long ways. The spinal column is a small target, and when you're shooting from the side it's not located where many hunters imagine it to be. (Rather than being in the middle of the neck vertically, it's about two-thirds of the way up—but not exactly.) From the front, the spinal column is an extremely small target horizontally. Vertically, it's not much better; you'd want to clear the top of the deer's back, but still aim below the deer's head. Even when deer

Heart-lung area of a deer standing broadside. Results in a quick, humane kill; damages very little meat. The best shot for bow-hunters.

Heart-lung area of a deer standing broadside, but quartering away from you. Bullet will go through the heart-lung area, and will probably strike the inner surface of the opposite shoulder. Results in a quick, humane kill. Damages meat on the opposite shoulder.

Heart-lung area of a deer standing broadside, but angled toward you. Aim for the shoulder; if you aim farther back, the bullet will only damage one lung.

High on the shoulder of a deer standing broadside. Will break one or both shoulders, transmit massive shock, and do serious damage to the deer's lungs. Could also damage a fair amount of shoulder meat. (With a lighter caliber and a larger deer, there's some risk that the bullet could expand when it hits the shoulder bone, and then not penetrate quite enough.) Good choice when you're near a property line and you wouldn't be able to trail a wounded deer onto the adjacent property.

Front and center on a deer facing directly toward you. Too low, and your bullet will graze the deer's belly. Too high, and you'll damage those tasty backstraps along either side of the spine. Aim right for the middle. Even then, too much penetration could leave you with a messy field-dressing job. You may want to wait for the deer to turn a bit to one side.

Neck shot from the side. Use with caution. You're aiming at a very small target that's difficult to locate precisely.

are feeding calmly they tend to move their head and neck around more than the rest of their body—often when you least expect it.

- **Don't aim specifically for a deer's heart.** It's a small target, and a little lower and farther forward than most hunters realize. If your aim is a little off, you'll graze the deer's belly or chest or shoot its front legs. Not good. Instead, aim more generally for the entire heart-lung area.

These photos show where you should aim. To keep things simple, we've used a 3D archery target. For this section, at least, we can truthfully say that no deer were harmed in the making of these photos.

Think in 3D, and Shoot the Center of the Basketball

From these examples, you can see that it's important to think in 3D. Deer aren't two-dimensional objects, and they won't always be standing precisely broadside.

I often tell new hunters to visualize a deer's lungs as a basketball that's floating in between the deer's shoulders, centered just about vertically in its body. About half of the basketball is located between the deer's shoulders. The other half extends beyond the rear of its shoulders; it's right inside the ribs.

If you shoot the basketball, you've got your deer. But remember that old "aim small, miss small" idea? Don't just aim for the basketball. Aim for the center of the basketball.

If you shoot the center of the basketball, you've got your deer.

A .243 angled from the rearward, through the heart-lung area and into the opposite shoulder. This deer dropped in its tracks. Only a small amount of meat was damaged.

A deer's lungs, of course, are not perfectly spherical. Still, it's a good way to visualize this. And that's about how big the lungs are on an average deer. (The lungs of an elk or moose are more the size of a beach ball.)

A deer's heart, however, is about the size of a baseball—or maybe a softball if it's a really large deer. That's why you're much better off aiming for the general heart-lung area. When you do, you may end up damaging the heart and aorta, too. And if you put a bullet or arrow anywhere into the "basketball," that deer is destined for your dinner table.

What Your Butcher Already Knows

Finally, let's take a look at the results you'll get with some of these shots. We know this may not be very appetizing, but sometimes a picture really is worth a thousand words.

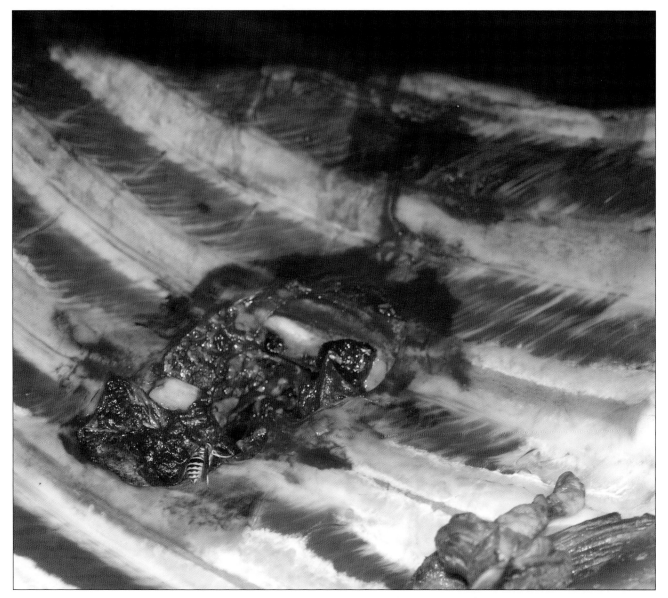

A .243 broadside, through the heart-lung area. This deer dropped after only a few paces and almost no meat was damaged. A larger caliber would have achieved similar results, and without any more damage. (If you're butchering when it's warm out, beware of wasps that may be attracted by the smell of meat.)

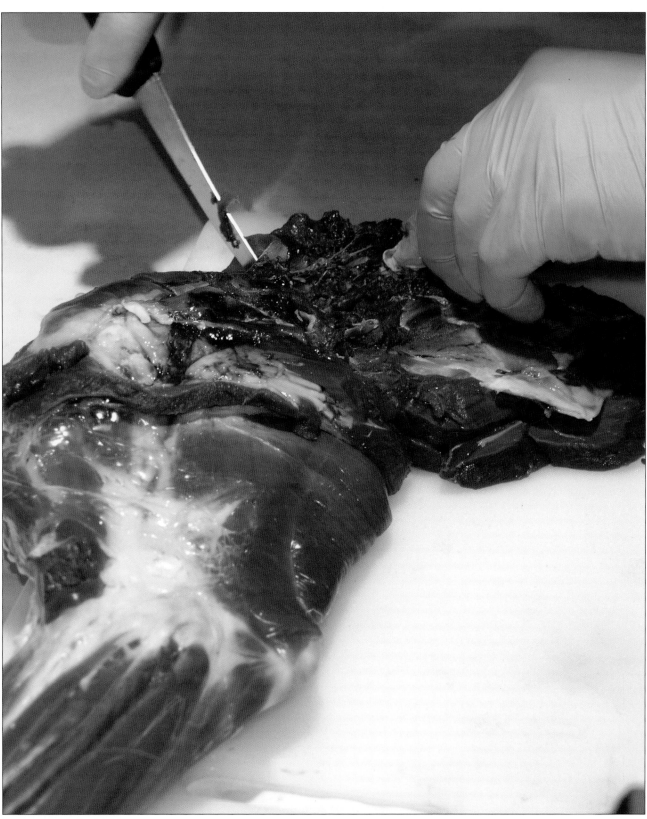

A shoulder shot with a .300 Winchester Magnum. This deer dropped in its tracks. We lost only a few more ounces of venison than we did when making a similar shot with a .243.

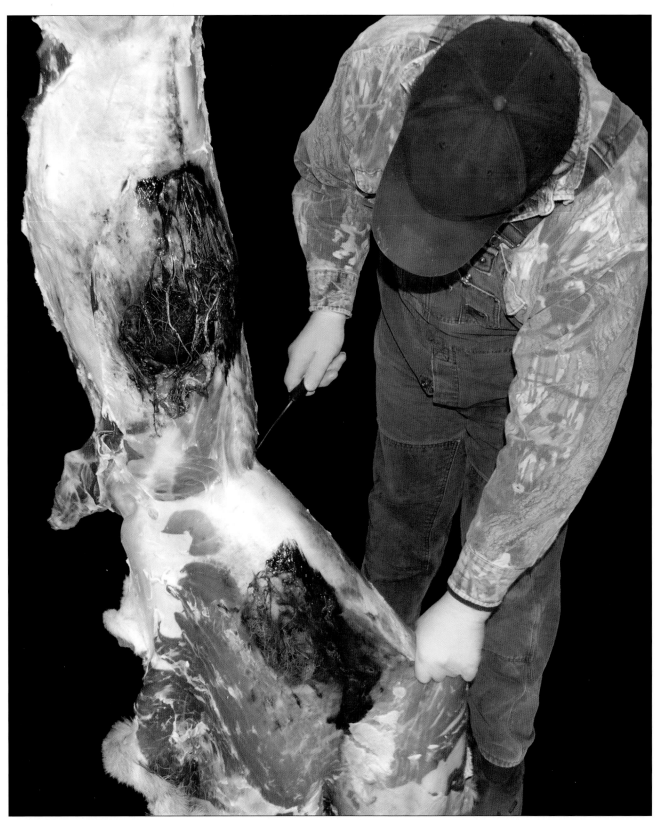

A spine shot with a .300 Winchester Magnum. Despite the dramatic damage, this deer didn't expire instantly. No backstraps for us this time; six inches lower and things would have been different.

CHAPTER 4

Field-Dressing Your Deer

Photo courtesy of Dan Schmidt

You made a good shot and your deer is down. First, approach it cautiously. Make sure your deer is down for good. Use a second shot if it's the humane thing to do.

Approaching from the side away from the hooves, touch the deer with your foot to make sure it's dead. Then use your bow or the end of your rifle barrel to touch the deer's eye; if the deer doesn't blink, you know it's dead.

If your deer is down but still alive, don't try to quickly step in and cut its throat. Even if it's taking its last few breaths, its hooves could be faster than your knife. Again, use a second shot into the heart-lung area if it's the humane thing to do.

Calm Down and Get Ready

Once you're certain your deer is down for good, tag it so it's officially yours. Go ahead and take a few pictures if you like. If your hands are shaking, take a few moments to relax and calm down. A delay of a minute or two won't matter.

While you're collecting your thoughts, look around and assess the terrain. If you can, pick a spot where gravity will make your job easier. Maneuver your deer so the head is slightly downhill—ideally, in a slight depression to keep the deer from rolling on its side. Later, after the first few steps, you'll turn the deer around so its head is slightly uphill.

If you're hunting with a friend, you can have them hold the deer's legs out of the way. Even then the job will be easier if you can take advantage of the terrain.

Get out some string, your knife and any other tools you'll use. Make sure everything is laid out and ready before you put on your gloves.

If you're hunting in cold weather, you may want to peel off a few layers. This will be hot work and you won't want to get your favorite hunting jacket all bloody.

Be safe and plan for success. If you're out during gun season, always wear a blaze orange vest or shirt under your jacket. You won't want to be wearing your favorite tan shirt while you're bent over field-dressing your deer.

Field-Dressing Myths

Before you snap on your gloves and get started, here are a few things to not do:

- **Don't cut off the tarsal glands.** These scent glands are visible as small dark patches on the inside of the deer's hind legs. Although some hunters slice them off to avoid contaminating the meat, there's no better way to do exactly that than to slice into them and then use the same knife to field-dress and butcher your deer. Instead, just leave these scent glands alone.

- **Don't cut the deer's throat.** In most cases, your bullet or arrow will have already taken care of the bleeding. That's especially true if you've made a good shot in the heart-lung area. Cutting the throat will only provide an extra entry-way for dirt and germs. And if you shot a trophy buck that you'd like to have mounted, cutting its throat will damage the hide beyond repair.

- **Don't open the deer from its chin to its tail.** Only do this to speed cooling in extremely warm weather. Normally you can field-dress your deer without even opening the sternum. You'll need to reach farther up inside the rib cage for a few steps, but you'll also provide fewer opportunities for dirt, insects and bacteria to contaminate your venison.

Make Your First Cuts

You'll hear different opinions about the best place to start; some prefer to start near the sternum or midway along the abdomen. That gets you off to a good start; it's a real confidence-builder when you make rapid progress during your first few cuts.

Instead, however, we suggest beginning a bit farther toward the rear. Here's why. If you begin

BOWHUNTING SAFETY TIP:
FIND YOUR BROADHEAD

Before we continue, here's a final safety warning. If you're bowhunting, and if you've recovered your arrow, check to make sure the broadhead is still intact. And if you're not sure, be careful when you're working near the area where the arrow passed through your deer.

This is especially important if you're using expanding broadheads, or broadheads with detachable blades. If part of a broadhead is still in the deer, you won't want to unexpectedly find it with your hand during these next few steps.

Even if you're *not* bowhunting, it's always a good idea to look your deer over for signs of old wounds. On rare occasions, unlucky hunters have been cut by someone else's broadhead as they're field-dressing their deer.

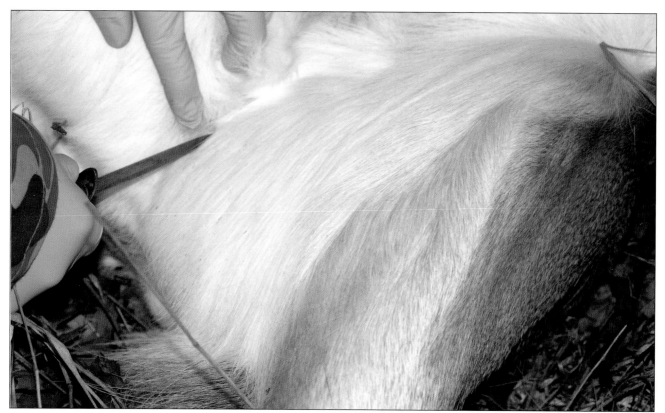

You have to start somewhere.

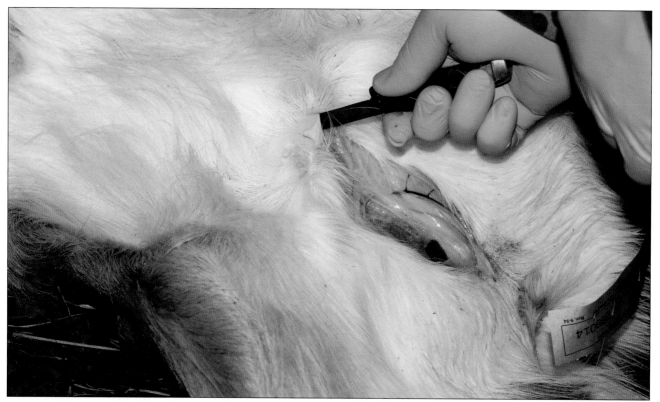

Cut through the udder of a dry doe, but around the udder of lactating doe.

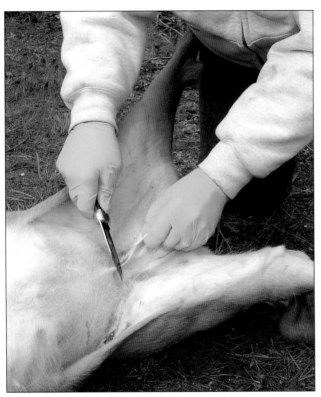

When field-dressing a buck, you'll first cut through this fold of skin.

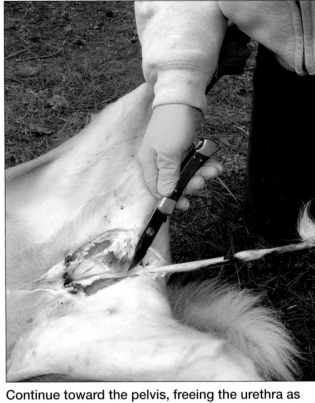

Continue toward the pelvis, freeing the urethra as you go.

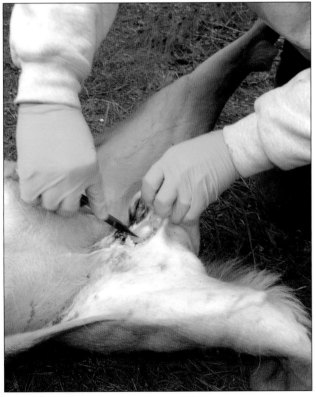

Next, cut around both sides of the scrotum.

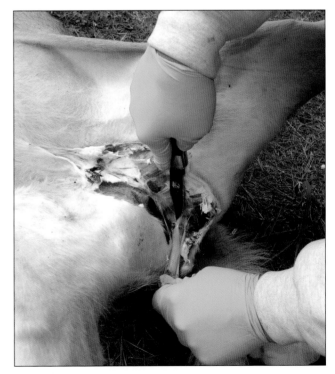

You've freed the buck's urethra; from here on, the remaining steps will be pretty much the same for either a buck or a doe.

Continue toward the pelvis (doe).

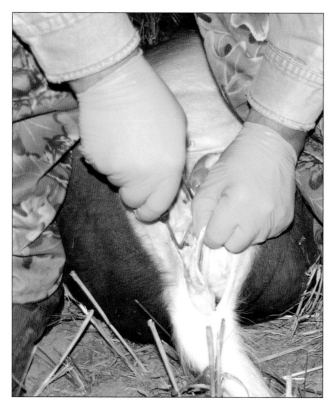

Cut carefully, and take your time.

opening the abdomen farther forward, there's a chance the internal organs could bulge out and rearward, spilling over the area you'd like to work on next. That's especially likely if the deer has been browsing recently.

The small, precise cuts you'll make in the anal and genital areas are much easier if the deer is on its back with its hindquarters slightly elevated. (After these first few steps, you'll reposition the deer so its head is slightly uphill.) And by starting here first, you'll be getting the more difficult and unpleasant parts of the job out of the way first. After that it only gets easier.

For all these reasons we suggest this area as a good place to begin. Let's get started. In general, these steps are similar for either a buck or a doe. There are just a few differences and we'll point them out as we go along.

For a doe, your approach to this step will vary depending on whether you shot a lactating doe or a dry doe. On a dry doe like the one on page 73, cut from the rear of the deer forward, right through the center of the udder. On a lactating doe, cut around each side of the udder and remove it carefully. Any warm milk spilled on your venison can give the meat a sour flavor. (If you hunt in an area where you're required to leave proof of gender attached to the carcass at registration, you may need to leave a small portion of the udder attached.)

When field-dressing a buck, you won't need to cut into the genitals or cut through them; just cut them free from the abdomen and lay them aside before you continue. (Or, if you're hunting in a state that requires proof of gender at registration, just cut around one side and leave the genitals attached to the hide.)

First, grasp the penis and pull it toward the rear. Then cut through the fold of skin that holds it against the abdomen.

Next, cut alongside both sides of the scrotum. With your other hand, continue pulling the

QUARTER YOUR DEER IN THE FIELD?

This is the technique usually used for elk and moose; even after field-dressing, these animals would be too large and heavy to drag out in one piece. The pieces left after quartering will still be plenty heavy enough. Although deer are smaller, it might still make sense to quarter your deer in the field when the terrain is rugged and you've downed a deer miles from the nearest road.

In some states, hunters use this technique for deer or antelope so they can keep meat from spoiling in the heat. If they can quarter the animal and fit all of the pieces in a cooler with some ice, they're set.

In other states, however, this technique wouldn't even be legal. Hunters in many states are required to bring their deer in relatively intact for registration. They can field-dress them, but that's about it.

This technique also has a few other disadvantages. It can be messy, and at best it exposes a lot more surfaces to dirt, hair, leaves, and other contamination. Spoilage begins on those exposed surfaces, not deep inside the meat. While you could certainly cover the pieces with cheesecloth or some other material, deerhide makes an even better cover—especially when it's still attached to its original owner.

genitals upward and toward the rear as you cut.

Continue cutting toward the rear, freeing the urethra as you go. It's just under the skin; you'll follow it along the spine of the pelvis, all the way to where it enters the rear of the pelvis.

When you get there, your next step will be to free the anal tract. For now, however, let's go back and work on that doe. From here on, the remaining steps will be similar for either a buck or a doe.

For a doe, continue toward the pelvis in a similar fashion. Slit through the meat until you find the spine of the pelvis.

Once you get to this point, withdraw your knife slightly. Now, your cut should be more shallow. You'll just be cutting through the skin and a small amount of connective tissue. Continue rearward a few more inches.

Next, cut around the buck's anal tract. For a doe, you'll need to cut around the anal, urinary and reproductive tracts.

Make your initial cut in the adjacent area and then use a slitting motion that pulls and cuts outward. Cut just under the skin, being careful to not puncture the colon or bladder.

On a warm, freshly killed deer, nothing in this area will feel firmly attached to the underlying muscle and bone; instead, it seems to stretch and move fluidly. Cut carefully in this area and take your time. Just in case your knife slips through unexpectedly, be careful to not cut toward yourself.

Even after you've done this a few times it's a little tricky. Try to cut with sort of a "coring" motion; your goal is to separate the anal tract from the surrounding tissue. Once you've cut through the skin on the outside and done just a little more "coring," you may be able to free the remaining connective tissue by grabbing and pulling. As necessary, make a few more cuts and try again.

Tie It Off (Optional)

After you finish cutting around the anus, you may want to tie a string around the lower end of the digestive tract. This makes it easier to avoid contaminating the meat with feces during the remaining steps—especially if you decide to not cut the pelvic bone. That's the next step, an optional one that we'll explain in a moment.

First make a loop like this…

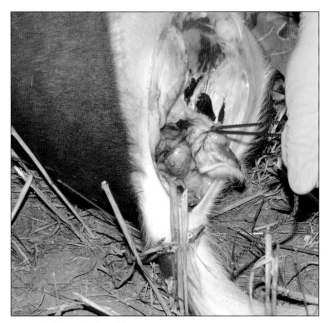

…and then tie it off.

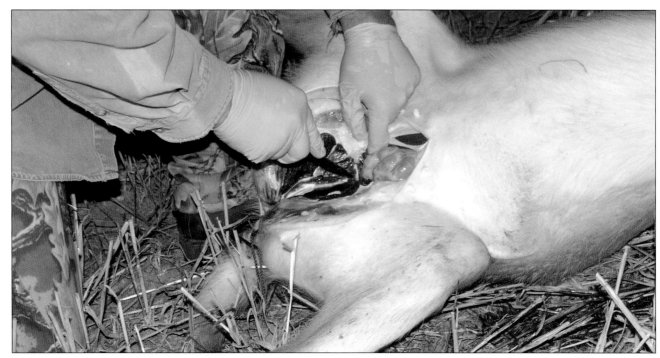

Getting ready to cut the pelvic bone.

Sawing through the pelvic bone.

Now you can pull the hindquarters apart, like this.

If you skip cutting the pelvic bone, you'll later thread the anal tract back through the pelvis rather than just lift it through the gap you've sawn. But if a few nice, dry deer pellets drop out into the abdominal cavity, don't panic. Just pick them out and toss them over your shoulder. Odds are that they've dropped onto the entrails you're about to remove anyway. If not, there's probably enough blood in the abdominal cavity to wash away any contamination. Later, you can also mop up more with a damp paper towel or a few handfuls of snow.

Cut Through the Pelvic Bone (Optional)

This step is optional. If the weather is warm, sawing through the pelvic bone will make it easier to open the abdominal cavity wide for quicker cooling. Otherwise, you may want to save this step until you get your deer home. If the abdominal cavity isn't open as wide, it will be less exposed to dirt, leaves and other contamination.

Start by making a careful cut in front of the pelvis to open a spot for your saw or knife. In a moment you'll cut through the pelvis, being careful to not puncture the bladder. Although it's possible to cut through the pelvis with a knife, it's much easier and safer to use a saw that's made specially for this purpose. It has a blunt "bumper" on the end that makes it less likely that you'll puncture any internal organs.

Use your saw to continue on through the pelvic bone. If you cut right through the center, it will only take a moment.

Once you're through, you'll be able to pull the hindquarters apart. Then you'll lift the intestinal tract—and, for a doe, the urinary and reproductive tracts—through this gap. You can do this now, or later when you're removing all the internal organs.

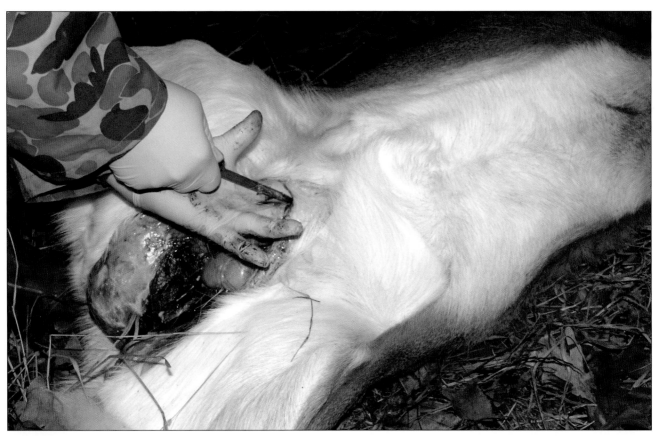

If you like, make this next cut in two steps.

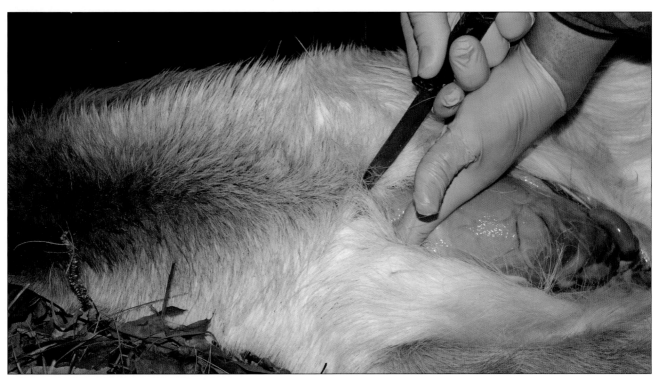

Hold your knife like this when you make this cut.

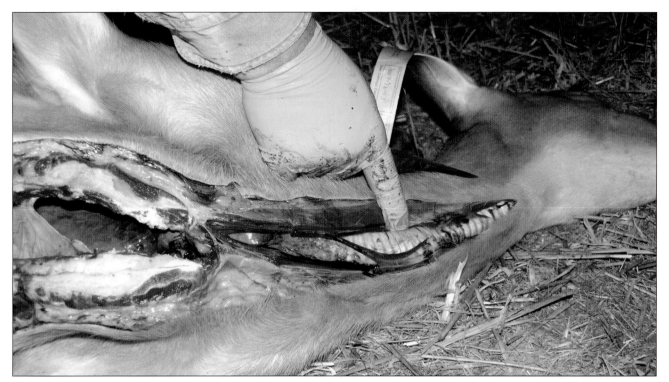

In warmer weather, you may want to cut through the underside of the neck to expose the trachea and esophagus.

If you don't cut the sternum, you'll need to reach in a little farther.

Slit the Abdomen

In this step, slit the abdomen all the way to the sternum. But before you do, now would be a good time to reposition your deer. Ideally, you had it positioned so the hindquarters were slightly elevated. From here on, gravity will be more helpful if your deer is positioned so its head is uphill.

Many hunters find that it's a little easier to slit the abdomen in two steps. First slit the skin, and then slit the layer of tissue underneath. After you have more practice, you can do both in a single step. Either way, it doesn't take long.

When slicing through the layer of tissue under the skin, hold your knife as shown on page 80.

With one finger on either side of the blade, cutting edge up, you'll be able to guide it away from the internal organs and smoothly slit the abdomen all the way to the sternum.

Many hunters prefer a knife with a special gut hook for this part of the job. But with a little practice you'll find that it's not really necessary. Just take your time and let your fingers push those internal organs aside as you guide the blade forward.

After some practice, this step only takes a few seconds. But if you're still learning, take your time. It's not a race, and the job could become messier if you puncture the deer's stomach or intestines.

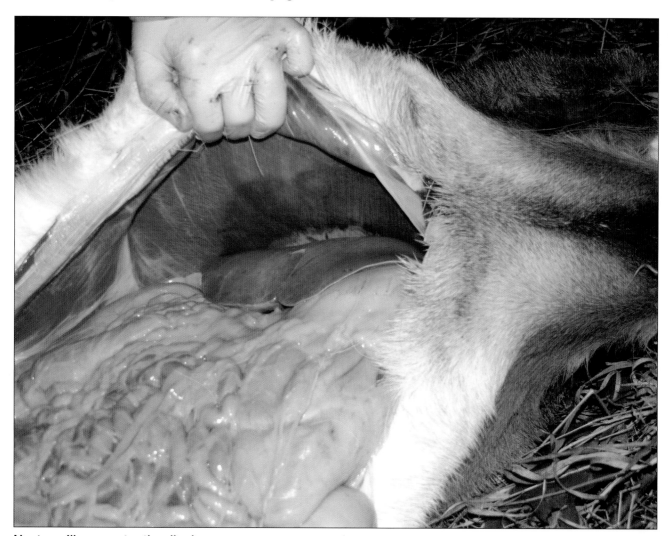

Next you'll encounter the diaphragm.

If that does happen, don't panic. Most of the leakage will end up on the entrails that you're about to remove. After that, there will probably still be a fair amount of blood in the abdominal cavity that you can use to sluice out any residual traces. And, again, you can mop up more later with a damp paper towel or a few handfuls of snow.

Cut Through the Sternum (Optional)

Here you have a number of options. Which you choose will depend on the weather and your personal preferences.

If it's cold out, you could stop cutting at the sternum. The less you open up your deer, the less opportunity there is for dirt, leaves and other contaminants to enter. That's especially important if you'll be dragging your deer farther to get it out of the woods.

The only disadvantage to not sawing through the sternum is that you'll need to reach in a little farther to complete the next few steps. If you shoot an especially large deer, it's good to have long arms.

If it's warm, you may want to cut through the sternum so your deer will cool faster. (Plus, you won't need to reach in as far to cut the trachea and esophagus.) The easiest way to complete this step is with your special saw.

If it's really hot out, you may want to cut

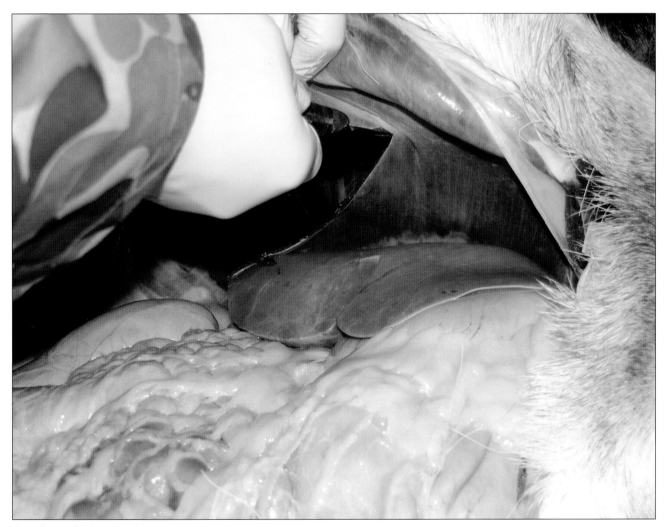

Cut through the diaphragm.

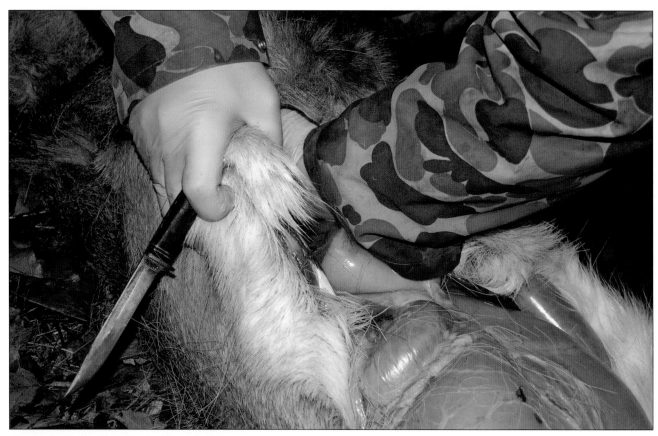

Reach in to locate the trachea and esophagus.

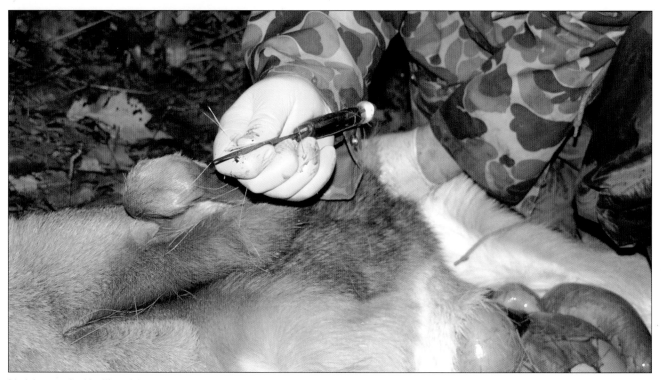

Hold your knife like this.

After you set your knife down, pull on the trachea and esophagus.

through the sternum and keep right on going. Split the underside of the neck to a point on the deer's throat that's just under the jawbone. Then cut the trachea (windpipe) and esophagus. For now, leave them attached to the internal organs.

This method makes for faster cooling. It does, however, have two big disadvantages. First, it exposes more of the carcass to dirt, leaves and other contamination. No matter how careful you are, this makes it harder to keep the carcass clean on the way home. Second, you'll obviously want to avoid this technique if you've just shot a trophy buck that you'd like to have mounted.

If it's warm out and you have a long drag to your vehicle, open your deer only as far as its sternum; that leaves a smaller opening for dirt and leaves. Then, once you get back to your vehicle, you can open it farther so it will cool more quickly on the drive home.

Cut the Diaphragm and Other Connective Tissue

Next you'll encounter the diaphragm. It's the thin layer of muscle and membrane that separates the lungs from the abdominal cavity. Before you can continue forward, you'll need to remove this obstacle.

As you hold the abdominal cavity open with one hand, reach in with your other hand to cut through the diaphragm. Continue cutting the diaphragm free along its entire circumference. After you do, you'll need to trim a few more pieces of connective tissue here and there.

Now pull the internal organs, including the heart and lungs, toward the rear as much as you can. You'll be able to pull the heart and lungs partly out of the rib cage, but not all the way. Unless you've done it earlier, you'll still need to cut the trachea and esophagus.

Remove the intestinal tract.

Finally. Time to pull all those innards out.

Cut the Trachea (Windpipe) and Esophagus

If you chose to cut through the sternum, continued on up the neck and cut the trachea and esophagus under the deer's chin, then you've already taken care of this step. Otherwise, you'll need to cut the trachea and esophagus free so you can remove the internal organs.

Even if you cut through the sternum, you'll need to reach way in to complete this step. If you haven't, you'll be in above your elbows—almost to your shoulder.

First, reach in with your "non-knife" hand. Feel around until you've located the trachea and esophagus where they enter the chest. You'll

know when you've found them. They'll feel like two hoses. The trachea has ridges on it, and the esophagus is smoother. In the same bundle, there are also some large blood vessels.

You may not be able to feel all these details; if you can feel those bumpy ridges on the trachea, you'll know you're in the right neighborhood. Get a good grip on this whole bundle.

In your other hand, hold your knife as shown on page 84. A grip like this will allow you to cut the trachea and windpipe with less chance of cutting yourself. Here's one time when a small, simple knife definitely works better than a large knife with a guthook.

Now slide your knife into position, right next

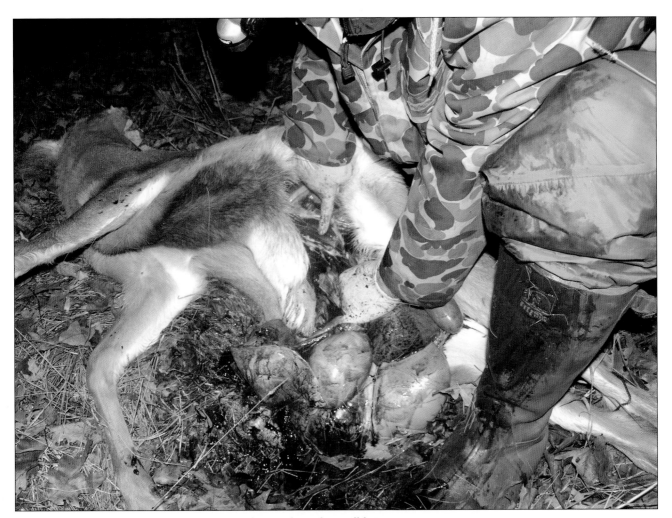

You can remove the tenderloins now or leave them in until later.

to where you're holding onto the trachea and esophagus. As you sever them both, be careful to not sever any fingers.

Keep a tight grip on the trachea and esophagus as you sever them. Once your knife goes through, pull your knife hand out and set your knife down. Do this before you begin pulling.

By the way, make a mental note of where you put your knife. Don't, however, stick it in the ground so it will be easier to find. When I got in that habit, it took me a few years to figure out why my knife was getting dull so fast.

Now pull hard on the trachea and esophagus. If necessary, use both hands. Pull them all the

Lift the deer and pour out any remaining blood.

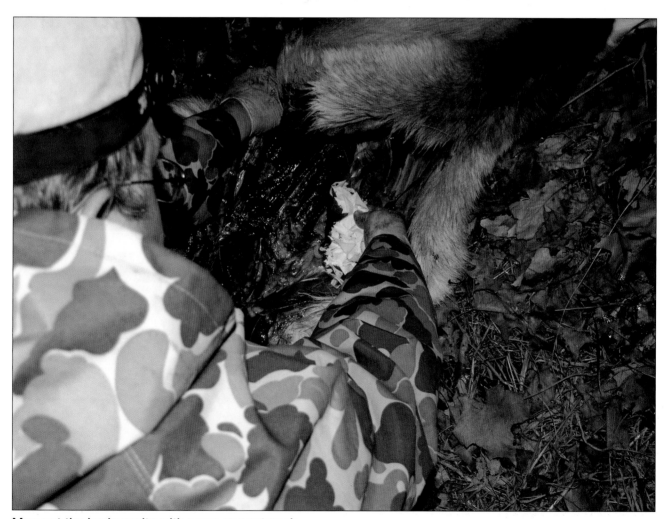

Mop out the body cavity with some paper towels.

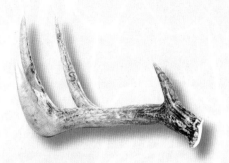

SHARE YOUR VENISON WITH THE NEEDY

We'd like you to keep reading and learn how to finish the job. When you do, your venison will be delicious. It's something you can take pride in, and we wouldn't blame you if you wanted to share a few steaks with your friends and neighbors.

Some day, however, you might also take an opportunity to share some of your venison with the needy. If you do, your work will be done after you've finished field-dressing your deer; you can just drop it off at the nearest participating processor.

To learn more about how these programs work where you live, search on the web for "deer donation" or "venison donation." Or, contact your local butcher shop or your state's Department of Natural Resources.

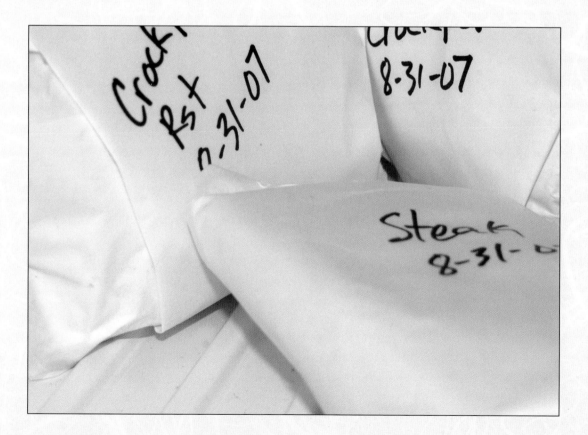

way out, and pull the heart and lungs along with them.

If you pull hard and nothing budges, just reach back in and do a little more trimming, then try again.

There. That was the tough part. You're almost done. Next, you just need to free the internal organs the rest of the way, dump them out, and perhaps do a bit of final clean-up.

Free the Internal Organs

If you keep pulling rearward on the trachea and esophagus, most of the internal organs will come free fairly easily. Chances are good, however, that you may still need to cut a few bits of connective tissue here and there. As you do, be careful not to cut the bladder or intestines.

If you haven't already done so, thread the intestinal tract and urethra through the pelvis. Or, if you sawed through the pelvis, just lift them through the center of the pelvis, right where you sawed.

Once you've cut through the last few bits of connective tissue, you'll be able to pull all of the internal organs out in one big pile. This is what's known informally as a "gut pile."

Congratulations! The hard part is done.

Remove the Tenderloins, Heart, and Liver (Optional)

The tenderloins are probably the choicest cut of meat on the entire deer. They're found on the inside of the abdominal cavity, just behind the shoulders and to either side of the spine. Some hunters like to remove them now so they won't dry out.

To remove them, cut the attachment at either end of the muscle. Then grab the tenderloin and pull hard. We usually wait and do this after we get back; that way it's one less thing to worry about on the way home. It's up to you.

If you like, you can also save the heart and liver. Some hunters carry a bread bag or a resealable plastic bag just for this purpose.

Pour and Mop

There will still be a surprising amount of blood in the deer's body cavity. Lift the front legs, turn the deer over and dump it out. Then do it again. This time keep the open side up and pour toward the rear.

This step can be awkward, especially with a large deer. Try it a couple of times, shaking and sloshing at different angles. Even when a lot of blood comes out on the first pour, there may still be more.

If you can, wipe the body cavity out with paper towels or snow. If all you have handy is grass or leaves, you'll probably want to skip it. Instead of making things cleaner, you could end up leaving bits of grass, dirt and leaves sticking to inside of the body cavity.

The exception might be for a gut-shot deer or if you accidentally punctured the intestines while field-dressing your deer. Then it might be a matter of using fresh, clean grass to wipe away some partially digested grass. Do what seems appropriate. You may even want to trim away any areas that won't come clean; this can be especially important in warm weather.

Later, once you're out of the woods, you can always use some damp paper towels to wipe out the inside of the body cavity more thoroughly.

Should you wash your deer?

What about cleaning out your deer's body cavity more thoroughly, either now or after you get home? Should you even wash your deer?

Some say never. After all, a moist carcass provides a perfect breeding ground for bacteria; your venison is less likely to spoil if you keep it dry. Others say always. After all, your venison is less likely to spoil if you keep it clean. Plus, a dunking in cold water can help quick-chill the carcass.

We say… It depends. Use your judgment and consider whether a thorough washing is more likely to help or hurt.

If, however, you find yourself dealing with a gut-shot deer, hose out the abdominal cavity as quickly and thoroughly as you can. Skin the deer immediately. Adjacent to the exit wound, you may find chunks of stomach matter lodged between the hide and the meat. Trim away any areas that are questionable, and remember that most of the edible meat has not been in contact with the abdominal cavity or its contents.

In Camp and on the Way Home

Once you get your deer out of the woods, what happens next? And what if you'll be in deer camp for another week before starting a four-hour drive home?

Every situation is different, but here are some general guidelines:

- **In some camps, deer will inevitably freeze.** All you can do is try to avoid repeated freeze-and-thaw cycles. Try not to hang your deer in the sun. Hang it where it will be in the shade most of the day, just as you would when it's warmer.

- **In other camps, heat and insects are more of a problem.** Cheesecloth game bags and sprinkled pepper can only do so much to protect your venison. Be safe. Do whatever it takes to get your venison butchered and chilled before it spoils.

- **If your deer will hang for a few days in camp, it won't need more aging when you finally get it home.** Butcher it as soon as you can.

- **If you're lucky enough to get your deer early in the week, watch the weather.** Consider butchering your deer in camp, even if it means extra trips to town for more coolers and ice.

- **If it's warm and you have a long drive home, put your deer in the back of your truck with a few bags of ice inside its body cavity.** Lay a few more bags or blocks of ice beside it, and then throw a damp tarp over the whole works. Don't wrap it tightly; leave room for air to circulate. If you're driving more than a couple hours, stop occasionally for fresh ice. And if you're driving home with a deer in the back of your hatchback, station wagon or SUV, turn off the heat and turn on the air conditioning.

Hunting can be an enjoyable pursuit even when you don't bring home a deer. But once your pursuit ends in success, you now have the opportunity to keep or lose hundreds of dollars worth of prime venison.

Over the years we've heard too many rumors about deer that were proudly displayed on a camp's "buck pole" for just a little too long and ended up rotted, inedible and quietly dumped back in the woods somewhere.

Don't do that.

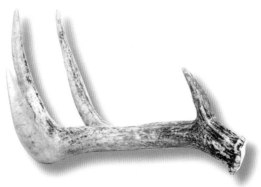

CHAPTER 5

You Got Your Deer Home. Now What?

Photo courtesy of Dan Schmidt

Once you get your deer home, what's next? The short answer to that question depends on the weather and the time of day:

- **If it's late and it's cool out...** Hang your deer up and work on it tomorrow.
- **If it's still early...** Why procrastinate? You can at least skin your deer now. The fresher a deer, the easier it is to skin. You can always stop there and finish the job tomorrow.
- **If it's warm...** Skin your deer so it cools more quickly. If it's really hot out, begin butchering; waiting even until morning could be risky.

By now you've probably noticed a recurring theme: Keep your venison cool and butcher your deer sooner rather than later.

Head Up or Head Down?

Once you arrive home, you'll want to get your deer off the ground. But should you hang it head up or head down? Either is okay; it all depends.

If you'll skin and butcher your deer soon, hang it from a gambrel right away. First, however, you'll need to remove the head and the lower legs; we'll show you how in a moment. (The exception, of course, would be if you've shot a buck and you'd like to save its head and cape for the taxidermist.)

Photo courtesy of Jacob Edson

Remember to place cardboard under the deer to catch any additional drainage.

Photo courtesy of Dan Schmidt

WHAT'S SO GREAT ABOUT "CAREFULLY AGED BEEF?"

First, keep in mind that most beef is not aged—unless, that is, you count any incidental "aging" that occurs during its brief trip to the supermarket. In modern packing plants, cattle are slaughtered, cut up and packaged, and on the way to your supermarket within a matter of hours. Most of that beef hits the shelf three or four days later.

Beef may not always be carefully aged, but it's always carefully marketed. A lot of that marketing, unfortunately, has influenced how we think about venison. So let's take a moment to consider this whole concept of "carefully aged beef."

Steaks made from aged beef cost a lot more, and they're only served in the finest restaurants. But what makes aged beef so special? And what makes it so expensive?

In theory, aging improves both the texture and flavor of beef. The chemistry behind this transformation involves naturally occurring enzymes that are in the meat itself. Over time, these enzymes break down muscle proteins. Most improvements in tenderness occur during the first week; the second week brings much smaller improvements.

Some fancy steakhouses, however, serve steaks that have been aged even longer. Although these steaks are a little more tender, a big part of the appeal is an enhanced flavor, one that some steak lovers describe as "stronger," "richer," or "more intense." Diners with less sophisticated palates, however, may not particularly care for this flavor; in some cases, they may feel that it's approaching "gamey."

As you peruse the menu at the very finest of these restaurants, you may even find that these overpriced steaks are described as being made from "dry aged beef." That's to distinguish it from beef that's been "wet aged." And wet aging, unfortunately, is just about what it sounds like.

This technique involves packing beef in plastic and storing it at 34 to 38° F for a week or more. It tenderizes the meat, but without greatly enhancing its flavor. Now, keep in mind that most beef isn't aged at all. But of the beef that is aged, today nearly all of it is "wet aged."

Dry aging is more like what home butchers try to do when they age venison. It's less common than wet aging because it means more work, more waste, and less profit. It also means refrigerating a huge inventory of prime beef carcasses for weeks on end.

What's more, dry aging isn't generally done in an ordinary walk-in cooler—or at least it shouldn't be. Temperature, humidity, and air flow are all carefully controlled. The beef is stored in a sterile environment that's kept between 34 and 38° F, with a humidity level of 50 to 75%. To slowly dry the meat, air is kept circulating continuously.

Although this drying is very controlled, it still results in a weight loss of 15 to 20%. Then, after an outer layer of dried crust—and sometimes a bit of green, fuzzy mold—has been trimmed away, the loss is even greater—sometimes up to 25%. The remaining meat will be sold for three or four times the price of "ordinary" steak. It has an intense flavor that's coveted by connoisseurs, but potentially a little too intense for the rest of us. It's especially tender, but only if it's cooked rare or medium-rare.

Just like ordinary beef, it would become tough if overcooked. Cooking time, in fact, has far more influence on tenderness than aging does; that's true for beef, and it's especially true for venison.

And one final note on aging… For safety reasons, pork is never aged. Neither is lamb, poultry, or pretty much any meat other than beef.

The whole process of carefully aging prime beef could actually be described as carefully controlled rotting. When you think about it, it's a pretty strange custom.

What about grass-fed beef?

Grain-fed, or grass-fed? At first glance, the answer to this question may not seem like it has much to do with aging. But when we're comparing venison and beef, the animal's diet is a big part of the overall "fat and flavor" picture.

Today, most beef cattle in North America are raised in feedlots. Of the rest, nearly all are fattened on grain during the final weeks before being slaughtered. Some people believe this improves the flavor of beef. We believe it removes the flavor of beef.

Grain-fed beef is bland. It gets most of its flavor from the extra fat, not from the meat itself. This is one more reason we shouldn't expect venison to taste like beef. These days, even beef doesn't taste like beef.

More recently, however, more and more consumers have been trying grass-fed beef. They want to eat healthy, and they've heard that grass-feed beef is leaner and more nutritious. Some, however, are trying it once or twice and then giving up it on.

Because grass-fed beef is leaner, it may not seem as tender and juicy as feedlot beef—especially if it' overcooked. Plus, people tasting grass-fed beef for the first time may find that its flavor seems stronger—almost like that of wild game.

One reason is that it's richer in Omega-3 acids—those "good fats" touted as a health benefit of fish. And so, by the way is venison. This nutritional difference is directly related to differences in the animals' diet.

This doesn't mean that either venison or grass-fed beef taste fishy. But they do have a different, richer flavor than grain-fed feedlot beef. And a deer from deep in the cedar swamps will probably taste different from a farm-country deer that's been supplementing its natural diet with alfalfa, corn, and soybeans.

Either of those deer, however, will taste great. The steaks may not taste "gamey," but neither will they taste like grain-fed beef. They'll have a flavor that doesn't need to be enhanced by aging.

If your deer is hanging by its hind legs, it will cool faster as heat radiates out from the open abdominal cavity. For that reason you may want to hang your deer head-down even if you're not going to butcher it immediately. To improve air circulation and speed cooling even further, saw through the sternum—and maybe even open the deer all the way up to the throat. Then prop the rib cage open with a stick. You can also buy a spreader that's designed especially for this purpose.

If you're not ready to start skinning and butchering, and if the temperature isn't a problem, you can hang your deer with a rope around its neck or antlers. Although a deer hung head-up may not cool quite as quickly, a potential advantage is that any remaining fluids will drain out of the body cavity without collecting in the

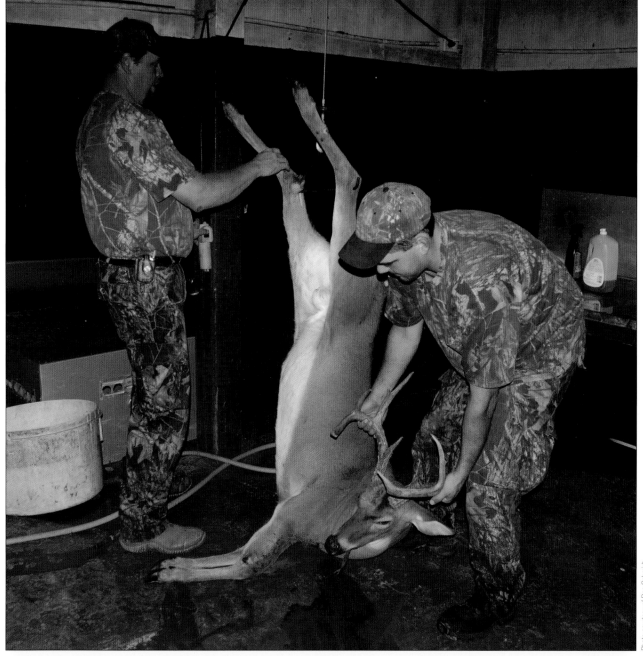

rib cage. In most cases, however, this isn't a problem anyway.

Myths About Aging Your Venison

Because these traditions are so deeply rooted, and because plenty of "experts" are sure to disagree, let's take a moment to debunk a few myths about aging your venison.

Here's the short version: Aging your venison won't significantly improve it. Aging your venison outdoors for more than a day or two will almost always make it taste worse. It could even turn your venison into a serious health hazard.

A Week on a Buck Pole?

In southern states, the weather is often warmer during deer season. When hunters return home at the end of the week, their venison is already butchered, packaged and frozen. That's a tradition to take pride in.

Farther north, however, you'll encounter a tradition whose roots are more cultural than culinary. Drive down any back road and you'll see a deer hanging from a tree in the front yard of a proud hunter. Drive a little farther and you may see a whole row of deer hanging from the "buck pole." Some hunters also call these structures "meat poles."

Unfortunately, aging deer for a week or more on a meat pole is not a good way to treat meat that you'd like to someday eat. As the weather changes during the week, the same deer hanging from the same tree could be subjected to a whole range of abuses:

- **When the temperature stays below freezing the carcass will freeze; not much "aging" will take place anyway.** It's just about impossible to skin a deer carcass when it's frozen; if you attempt it

How about a week on a buck pole?

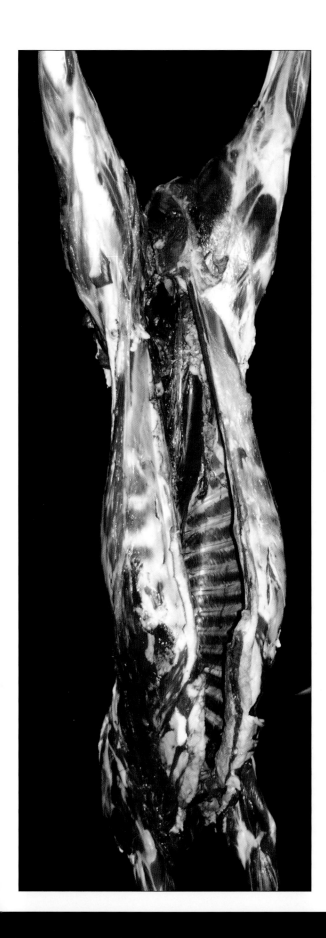

once, you'll never try again. And because deer hair is such good insulation, you may need to thaw the carcass all the way through before you can skin and butcher it. Then you'll need to freeze the meat for storage and thaw it one more time before eating it. That's not going to improve its flavor or texture.

- **When the temperature hovers around freezing, daily freeze-and-thaw cycles degrade the meat's flavor and make it dry and tough.** If the sun shines on the carcass for even part of the day, this could still happen when temperatures are below freezing.
- **When daytime temperatures climb into the 40s or 50s, the meat will still dry out.** (Unless there's rain in the forecast, and we don't even want to think about that.) But at these temperatures, your venison will also begin to spoil. If the temperature gets up into the 60s and 70s, even for an afternoon, then you've really got trouble. And again, if the sun shines on the carcass for even part of the day, all of this could be happening at what your thermometer tells you are much lower temperatures.

Aged, or Just Old?

The best advice we can give you, then, is to "first, do no harm." We recommend that you never age venison for more than a few days. Depending on the weather, you may not even want to do that. Here's why:

- **Aging only helps steaks, and maybe roasts.** The cuts destined for hamburger, sausage or stew meat won't benefit from aging. Plus, any meat that's going to be turned into hamburger or sausage will be tenderized in the grinder.
- **Even most beef isn't aged. It still tastes okay.** Because the marketing of aged beef influences how we think about venison,

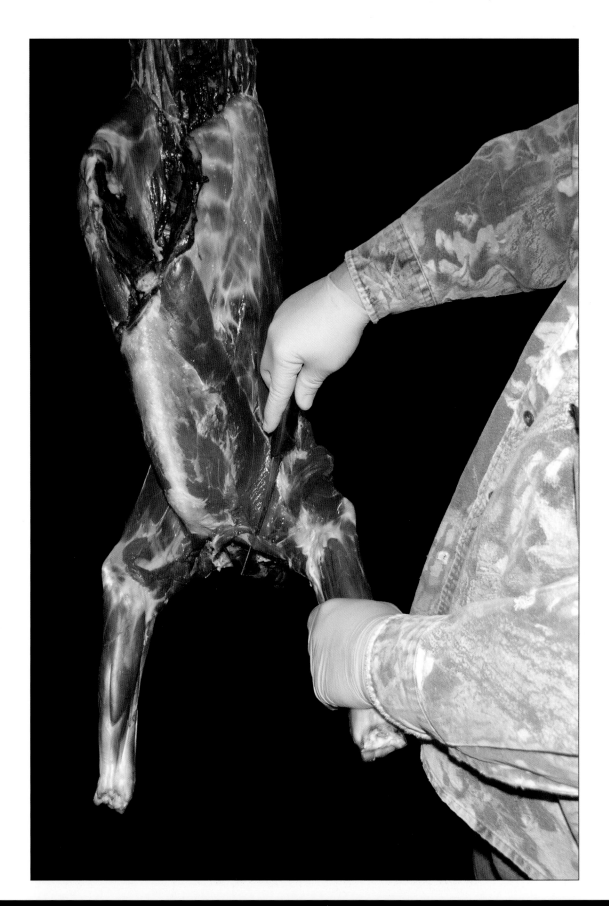

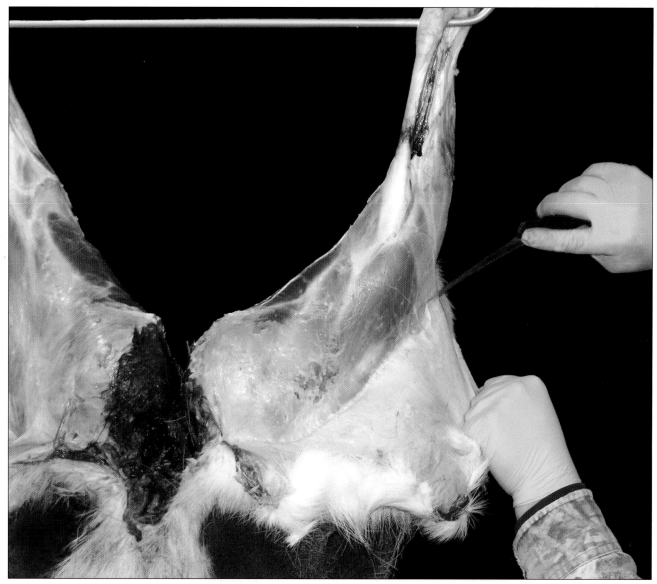

You could hang your deer from a gambrel right away.

it's important to remember that most beef, including steaks, is not aged. Today, most beef makes the trip from slaughterhouse to supermarket in about three days.

- **Pork, lamb and other meats aren't aged either.** Pork and poultry aren't aged because of safety concerns. Other meats, including venison, just plain don't need it.

- **Most venison is already tender.** It's possible that venison may become slightly more tender if it's aged a few days. Any differences, however, will be very subtle—and easily negated by even the slightest bit of overcooking.

- **Venison already tastes great.** Venison's flavor can't be greatly improved by aging. To our palates it already tastes better than beef.

- **Aging in uncontrolled conditions makes venison taste worse.** Well-intentioned "aging" is one of the biggest reasons for the "gamey" taste of wild game.

For these reasons, we recommend that you butcher your deer and get it in the freezer within three to four days, even in cool weather. If it's warm out, do whatever it takes to get that carcass cooled down fast. Then butcher it that day or the next day.

It's impossible to butcher a deer too soon. I've shot a number of deer early in the fall when the weather was quite warm. I had to skin and butcher them that night or the venison wouldn't have been safe. The steaks and roasts from those deer were invariably tender and delicious.

Keeping Your Venison Safe

We recommend that you read other books to learn more about food safety. But in the end it all comes down to touch, time and temperature:

- **Touch.** Keep it clean. Although some contaminants could be airborne or carried by insects, most get there by touch—usually during field dressing and transport. If the meat isn't contaminated, fewer microorganisms will make a home on your winter's supply of venison.

- **Time.** Don't give bacteria time to grow and multiply. If it's warm, cool your deer down fast. That way dangerous microorganisms have less time to begin colonizing your venison.
- **Temperature.** Life begins at 40. In this context, that means 40 degrees Fahrenheit. The warmer the air temperature, the more important it is to cool your deer down fast.

Working Safely

Enough about keeping your venison safe. Here are a few tips to help keep you safe:

- **Take your time.** The first few times, this will take a while. But please… Take your time. Otherwise, with fewer fingers, it will take even longer next time.
- **Don't get overconfident.** Later you'll gain confidence and work more quickly. That's when accidents are most likely to happen.

Instead, stay alert, stay aware and think consciously about every move you make.

- **If you're too tired, you're too tired.** We know… Just a few pages back we warned against waiting too long in warm weather. But sometimes too tired really *is* too tired. Get some ice on and in that deer, and get some rest before you start.

- **Work in an area with plenty of ventilation.** That way it will be easier to stay awake and alert. If you're using a propane heater to warm your garage, good ventilation becomes especially important.

- **Keep your work area cool, but not cold.** If your work area is too warm it's easy to become drowsy; you're also more likely to feel queasy from the smell of blood. If your work area is too cold, on the other hand, you'll be uncomfortable and stiff. That makes accidents more likely. Numb fingers are clumsy fingers. When you're using sharp knives that's not a good thing.

- **Cut away from yourself.** Pay attention to what you're doing and never cut toward your other hand or any part of your body. With some deer-butchering methods that's difficult to avoid. With the method we're showing you, you'll never need to cut toward yourself. Never.

- **Keep your knives sharp.** A sharp knife is safer; with a dull knife you'll push harder and mishaps are more likely.

- **Keep your floor clean and dry.** When hanging your deer, put some cardboard under it to soak up the blood. Later, you can move it out of the way when you're ready to start working. If necessary, use a little sand or cat litter for better traction. The last thing you need is a slippery floor when it's late, you're tired, and you're maneuvering around a heavy deer carcass while holding a sharp knife.

- **Lift safely.** Keep in mind these three tips:
    - Don't do more heavy lifting than nec-

essary. Use hoists and pulleys when lifting the entire carcass, or get someone to help.

- Lift with your legs, not with your back. We know you've heard it before, but it's still true. It's also a good idea to avoid bending or twisting when you lift.
- Wear old clothes. That way you'll hold heavy objects close to your body in a way that puts less stress on your back—even if it means hugging a damp deer carcass for a few seconds.

• **Finally, don't drink and butcher.** Or, at the very least, drink moderately. If you had a long day you'll be thirsty, and it's only natural that you and your friends will want to celebrate after a successful hunt. But we recommend that you save the serious celebrating until after the job is done. That's especially important when doing this the first few times. You need all your wits about you. You'll also be more likely to finish with all your fingers about you.

Make Your Final Preparations

Finally. It's almost time to get started. If you're prepared, it won't take long to go out to the garage, tape down some butcher's paper, and get out your knives, cutting boards and bowls. Forgetting anything? Review that checklist at the end of the chapter on Gearing Up and Getting Ready.

CHAPTER 6

Footless, Headless, and Up on the Gambrel

Photo courtesy of Dan Schmidt

In this chapter we'll:
- Remove the deer's head and lower legs.
- Expose the tendons in its rear legs.
- Hang it up on the gambrel.

If you just returned from a successful hunt, you may decide to complete these steps right now—either on the tailgate of your truck or in the grass and leaves at the edge of your driveway. Unless the weather is extremely warm, you can save the rest of the job until tomorrow.

If it's late and you're tired, you may not even want to begin these steps until tomorrow. Just hang the deer by its neck or its antlers and get a fresh start in the morning.

Tip: To avoid dulling your good knife, use a different knife for these steps. If you use your good knife, touch up the edge before continuing.

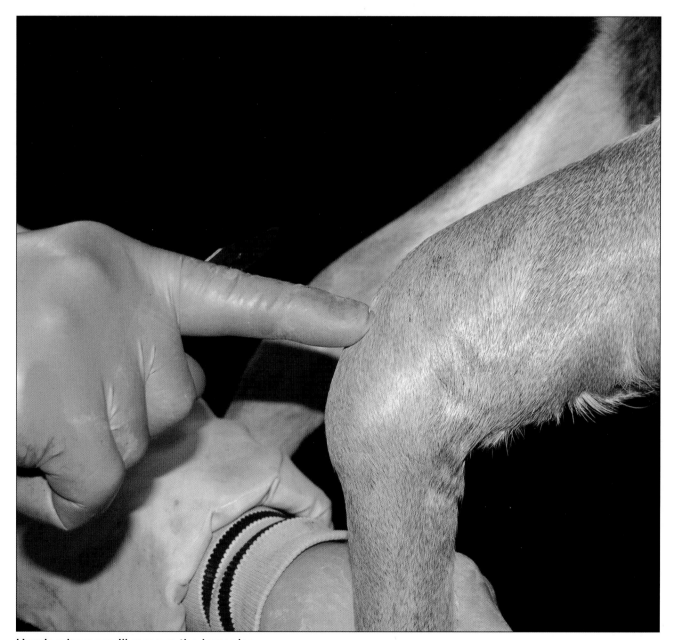

Here's where you'll remove the lower leg.

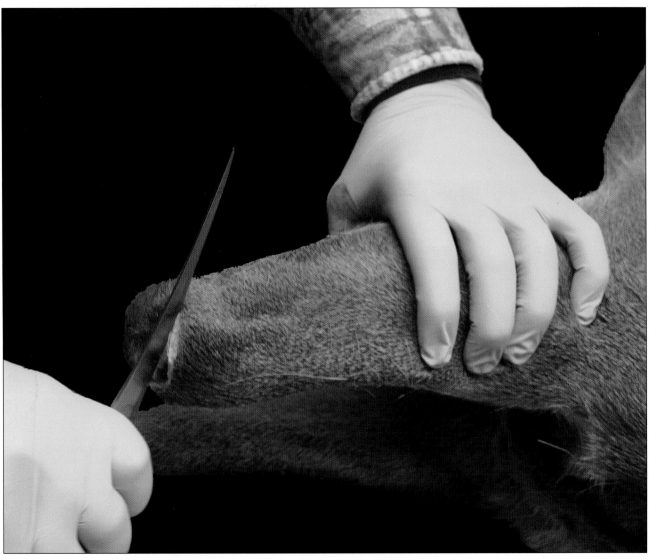

Begin your cut on the front side.

Remove the Front Lower Legs

In these photos, you'll see we took care of these steps right away when we arrived home. But if you've already hung up your deer by a rope around its neck or antlers, you can remove the lower part of its front legs while it's still hanging. Or, you can first lower the deer to the floor; in a minute, you'll be doing that anyway to remove its head. But first, cover the floor with a clean tarp or a few sheets of clean cardboard.

Cut in between the joints; if you cut in just the right spot you'll cut tendon, not bone. To get started, find the gap right in the middle of the joint. Deer don't have a kneecap; if you probe with your finger, you'll find a gap—almost a notch. That's where you'll cut.

The deer in this photo was a little stiff; its legs were partially frozen. If you can bend the leg past 90 degrees, this notch will be easier to identify. Start in the front and then cut the hide and the underlying tendons all the way around.

Grab the upper part of the leg in one hand and the lower part of the leg in the other. Twist firmly. You'll hear some crackling sounds, and then the twisting will suddenly get easier.

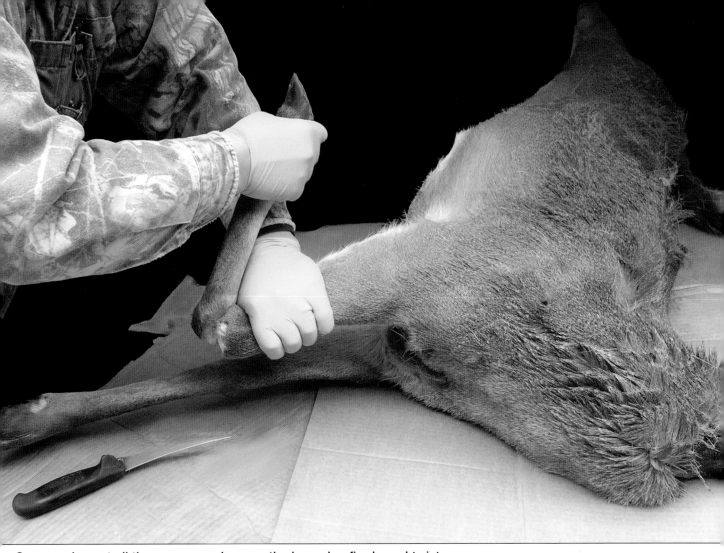

Once you've cut all the way around, grasp the lower leg firmly and twist.

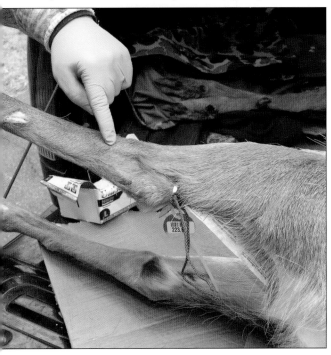

Here's where you'll remove the lower leg.

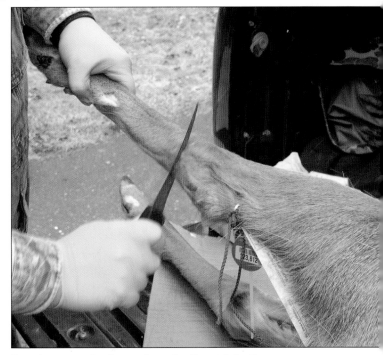

Cut down to the bone, but don't cut into it.

The leg may still be hanging on by the main tendon. If it is, reach in with your knife and make one additional cut to sever it. Then follow these same steps with the other front leg.

Remove the Rear Lower Legs

To remove the lower part of the rear legs, find the protruding bump at the deer's rear "knee" joint. Then measure downward the width of two fingers. That's where you'll cut. If you're uncertain, cut a little too low rather than too high.

Begin by cutting the hide and connective tissue all the way around, just as you did with the front legs. Cut down to the cartilage and bone, but no deeper.

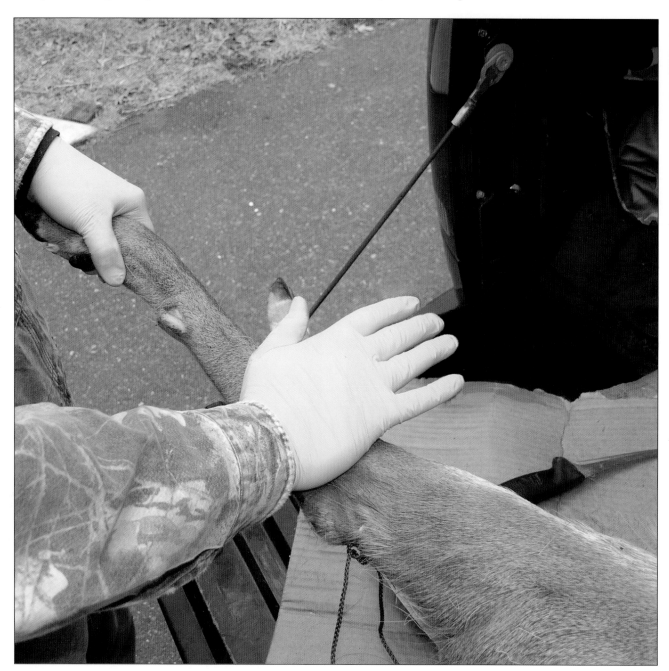

Bend the lower part of the leg to the outside.

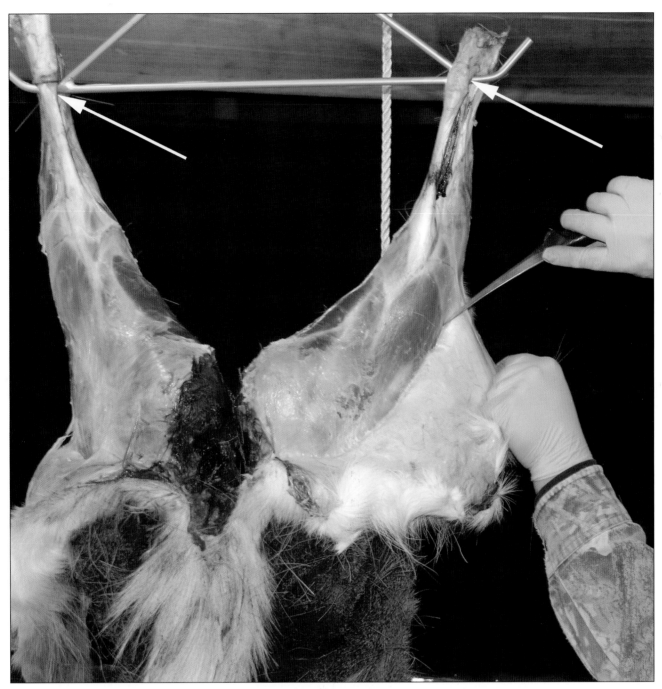

In a moment, you'll hang your deer by a gambrel inserted through these tendons.

Hold the upper part of the leg down with one hand. Then use your other hand to bend the lower part of the leg to the outside. You'll hear some snapping and crunching, and the lower leg may come completely free. Or, as with the front legs, you may need to sever the remaining tendon.

Expose the Hamstring Tendons and Hang Your Deer Back Up

Next, do some careful skinning and trimming to expose the hamstring tendons on the deer's rear legs. Then insert the ends of a gambrel between these tendons and the bones of the deer's upper leg.

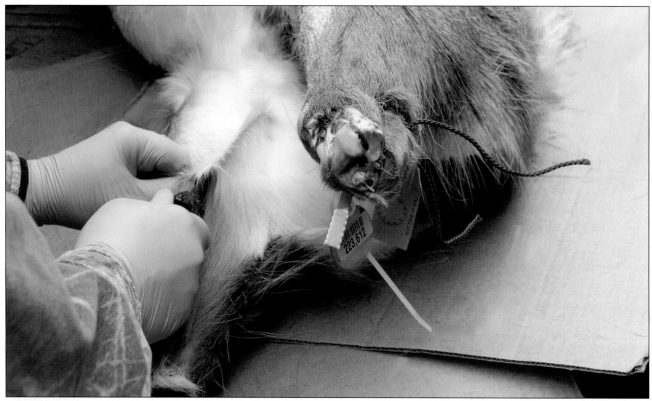

Start by making a slit up the inside of the rear leg.

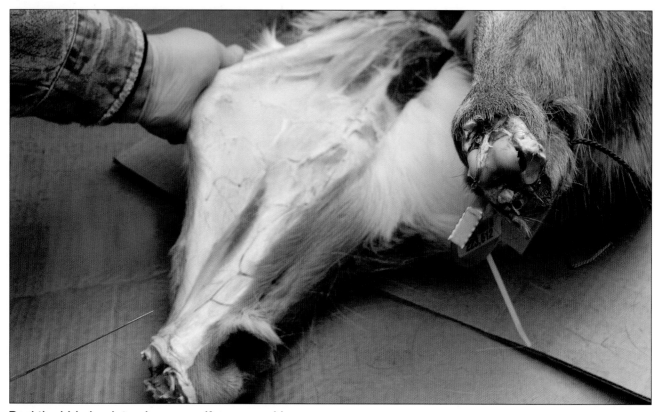

Peel the hide back to give yourself some working room.

To get started, slit up the inside of the rear leg. Start where you cut off the lower leg, and then cut all the way up until you reach the incision you made during field dressing.

Once you've done that, peel the hide away from the leg enough to give yourself some working room. You don't need to skin the rear leg completely. We'll work more on this area later.

Next, trim carefully around the joint to begin exposing the tendon. As you do, avoid the two scent glands. Be careful, too, to not cut through the tendon; if you do, you'll need to use some wire to hang the deer on the gambrel. If that happens, however, it's a simple repair. And when you're cutting nearby, you'll find that the tendon is quite tough.

Still, you could accidentally cut through it. It happens to the best of us. Or, you may have made your cut just a little bit too high when you removed the lower portion of the rear legs.

Dang! If you look closely, you'll see we've done exactly that. The end that's exposed should look more what you see on the other rear leg, the one in the upper-right corner of the photo on page 116.

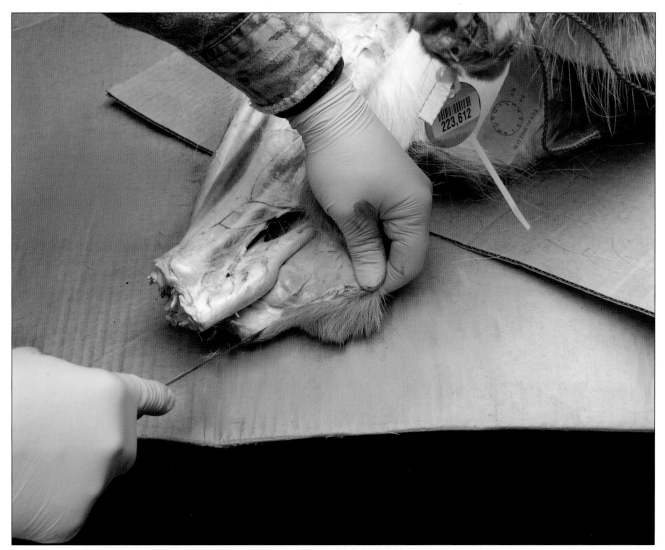

Next, trim carefully around the joint to begin exposing the tendon.

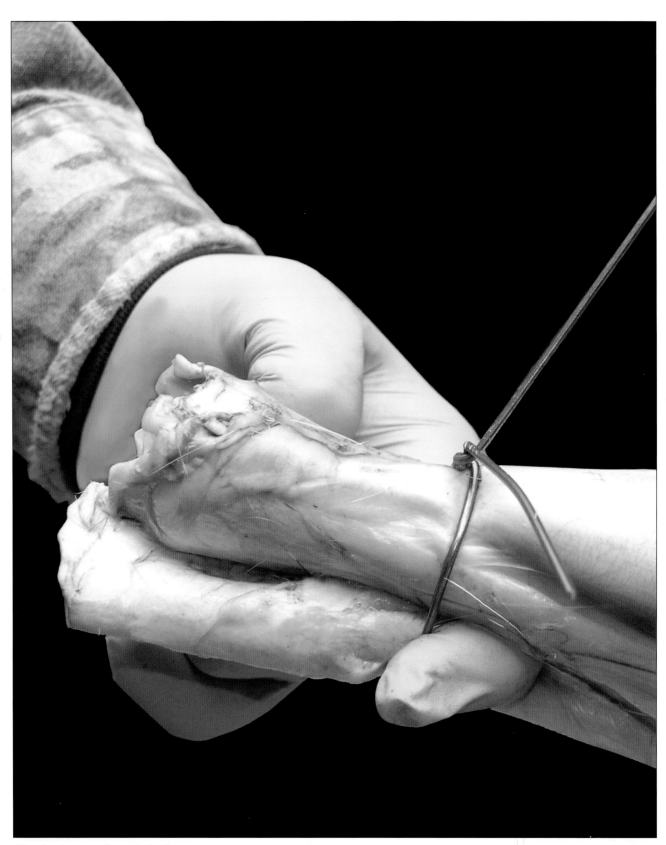

All wired up and ready to hang.

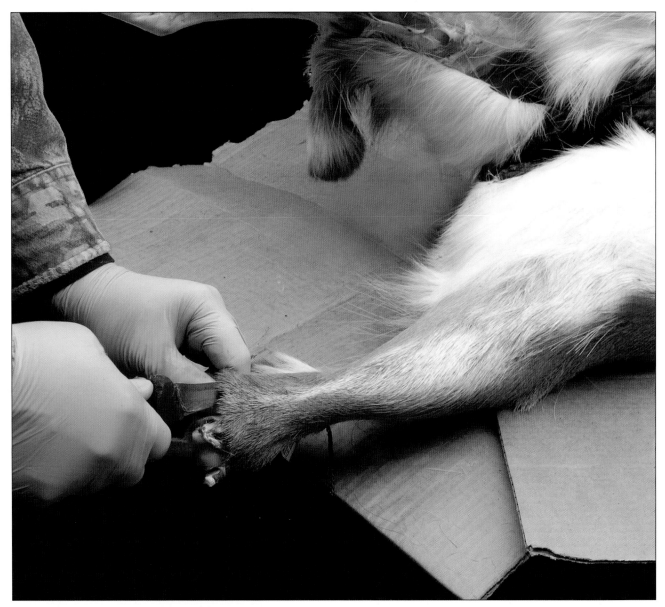

Now follow these same steps with the other leg.

Don't worry. This is an easy problem to solve. First, find some heavy-gauge wire that's still fairly soft; an old coat hanger works great. Cut off a piece about six or eight inches long. Wrap it around the spot you need to repair and then use a pliers to give the wire a few twists. If necessary, trim off the ends.

Once that's taken care of, you can follow these same steps to expose the hamstring tendon on the other leg.

Remove the Head

If you're butchering a trophy buck and you'd like to take this deer to the taxidermist, STOP. Don't complete this step now.

If this is a deer whose head you'd like mounted, you have a couple of different alternatives; we've described them in the final chapter. For now, however, let's assume this particular deer is just for eating and keep going.

The first time or two it's natural to feel a little

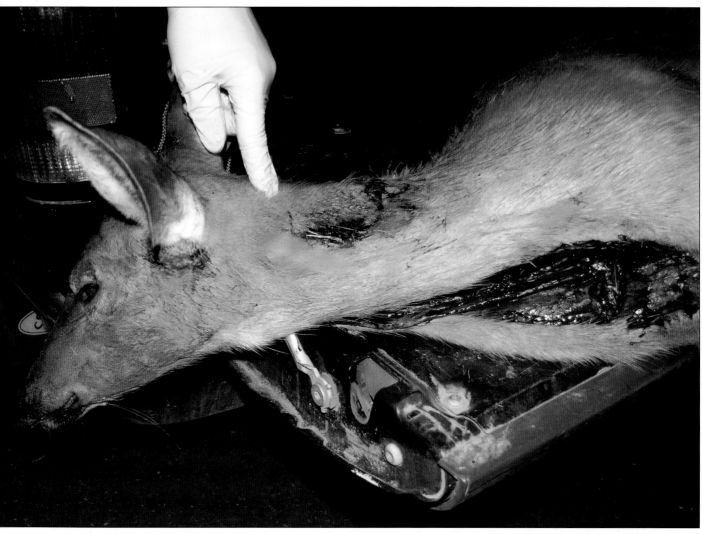

Make your cut right here.

squeamish about this step, but it will only take a moment. Let's take a deep breath and get it done.

Start your cut just behind the base of the skull. Then cut all the way around the deer's neck. As you do, slice in as far as the spine. Don't, however, dull your knife by pushing it forcefully against the vertebrae. In this first step, just expose them.

Once you do, you'll be able to see the vertebrae. Cut between the two vertebrae closest to the skull; that way you'll recover as much neck meat as possible.

When you begin cutting through the disc between these two vertebrae, you may be able to slice all the way through. But because of how the vertebrae are shaped, chances are good that you'll get partway through and encounter bone.

When you do, don't try to force it; that'll only dull your knife. Instead, set down your knife, get a firm grip on the deer's head, and twist. You'll hear a cracking, splintering sound, and then the head will be hanging loose.

It will probably still be attached by the spinal cord, and possibly by what remains of the disc you've been slicing through. Now pick up your knife again and cut through the spinal cord and any other material. It should be much easier.

Hang Your Deer Back Up

Hang your deer back up by its hind legs, inserting the gambrel through the slot you made behind the tendons. If you accidentally cut through a tendon during skinning or severed one of the rear legs too high, a little wire will solve the problem.

Now might be a good time to take a break...

If it's getting late, you can finish the job tomorrow. However, the fresher your deer, the easier skinning will be.

If there's danger of freezing you have extra incentive to skin your deer now. A frozen deer is just about impossible to skin. Without the skin the carcass may still freeze slightly, but that's okay as long as it doesn't freeze solid.

It's your call, but skinning won't take long. And once you're done you will have reached another natural stopping point.

Headless, footless, and up on the gambrel. If things didn't go well, you can solve the problem with a bit of wire.

CONSIDER CWD

If you're concerned about CWD, you have three options when it comes to removing the head:

· Leave the head on. It can stay on the carcass as you're butchering. When you're all done, you can leave it attached, and discard it with the bones and scraps.

· Use a different knife that you've reserved just for this purpose. Then go back to using your other knife.

· Keep using the same knife, but clean it with a bleach solution as soon as you're done with this step.

Even if they don't live in a CWD zone, many hunters use a separate knife for this step and for removing the lower legs. That way there's less chance of dulling your "good" knife before you begin skinning the deer. If you do use the same knife, you may want to touch up your edge before continuing.

Chronic Wasting Disease in North America

Areas with CWD infected Cervid populations

States/Provinces where CWD has been found in captive populations

Photo courtesy of Chronic Wasting Disease Alliance (www.cwd-info.org)

CHAPTER 7

Skinning Your Deer

Photo courtesy of Jacob Edson

This part of the job can seem a little overwhelming when you're doing it for the first time. But if you use a sharp knife and take it step-by-step, it's not bad.

Remember when you peeled back the skin to expose the tendons on the hind legs? That gave you a head start on the skinning process. It was also one of the toughest parts of the entire skinning job. The lower legs are probably the most difficult areas to skin. After that, the next most difficult will be the neck, brisket and shoulders.

If you continue with the back legs and work your way forward, stop before you go too far. If you don't, you'll soon be working with an inside-out hide draped over your head—like one of those old-time photographers crouching be-hind the camera. To avoid that problem, start with the front legs. They'll be a little tough to skin, but after that it gets easier.

Skin the Front Legs

First a tip for you northerners: Warm up your cold garage. Skinning this part of the deer is almost impossible if the carcass is even beginning to freeze. Because there's less mass to retain heat, the legs are the first part to freeze. Fortunately, if you can warm up your work area, they'll also thaw more quickly.

Here's an easy way to tell if the legs are fro-

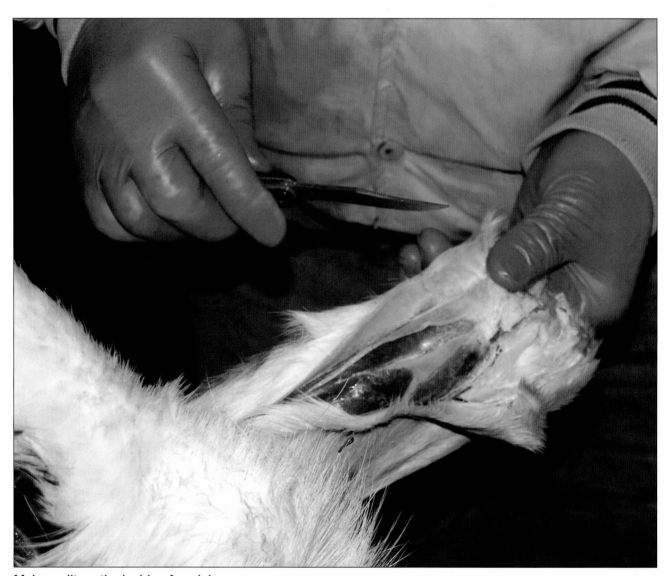

Make a slit up the inside of each leg.

This is one of the hardest parts.

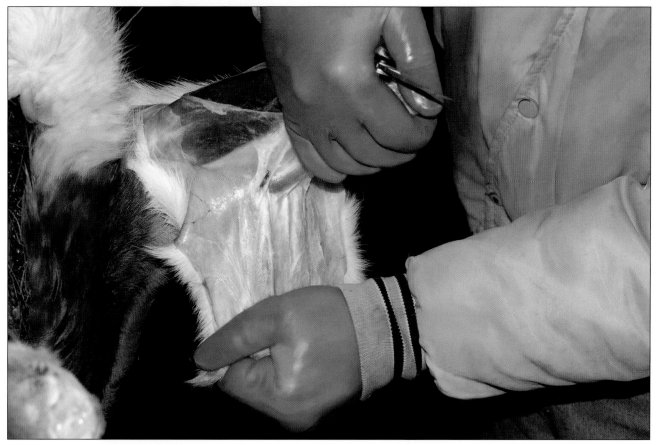

It gets easier as you go along.

zen. Grab one of the front legs with both hands. Then try twisting it, just as you'd twist a dish towel. If nothing moves, the legs are frozen. You'd better thaw them before you go further. If you can feel the skin moving slightly over the meat and bone beneath it, great. You're ready to start skinning.

Begin by making a slit up the inside of each leg. The underside of the leg is white; follow that inner boundary where the white meets the brown. Continue all the way up each leg until you reach the area where the leg meets the body.

Next, begin peeling pack the skin from around the legs. Just as you get started you'll encounter an area above the knee joint where the hide hangs on tight. Expect lots of cutting and very little pulling.

Hang in there; this part of the skinning job goes slowly for everyone. Take your time, make small cuts, and carefully separate the hide from the meat. Once you have the skin free all the way around and begin peeling upward, you'll notice a tendon that's attached near the joint. Cut this piece free from the hide, but leave it attached to the joint.

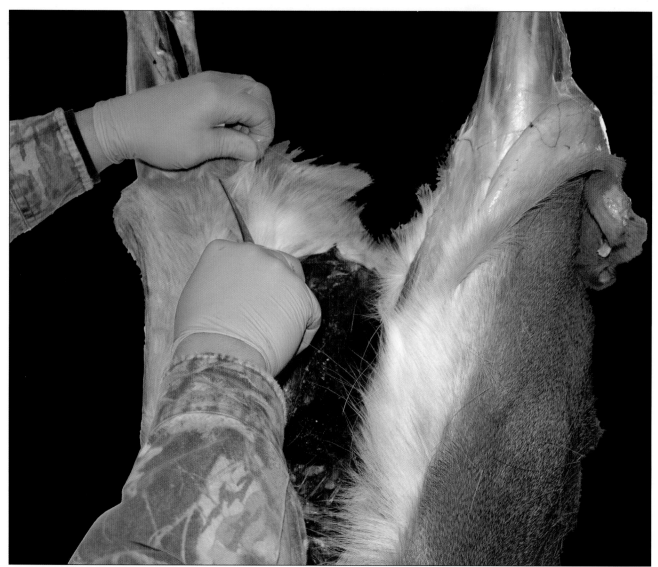

You already have a head start on the hind legs; just continue where you left off.

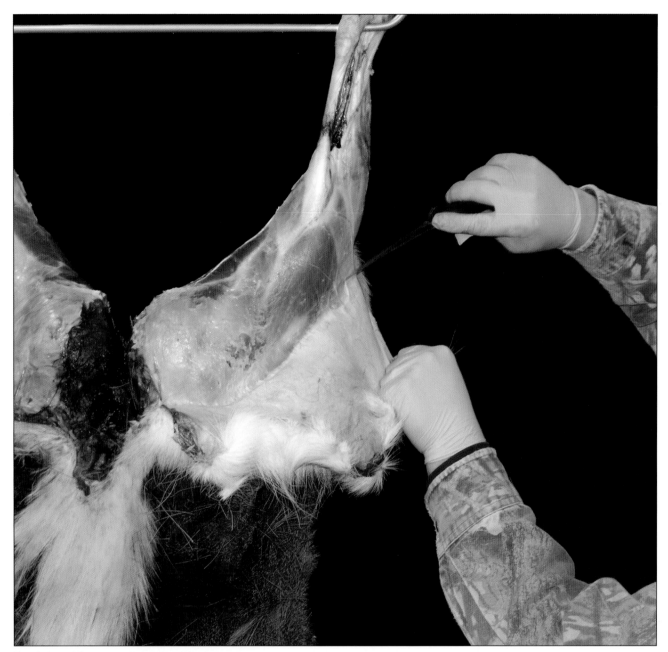

Peel the skin away from the hindquarters.

By now you'll have more of a flap free. Continue peeling upward. The skin will be easier to remove as you get farther up the leg. Keep going until you free the hide all the way up to where the leg meets the body. Then do the other front leg in a similar fashion.

Next, we'll finish the hind legs and work our way back down to this area.

Finish Skinning the Hind Legs

Earlier you exposed the hamstring tendons so you could hang your deer from a gambrel. Next, simply extend that same slit along the inside of the rear leg, just as you did with the front legs. Then pull and peel the skin away from the hindquarters.

On most deer, the skin comes free more easily

Pull the hide downward along either side of the tail.

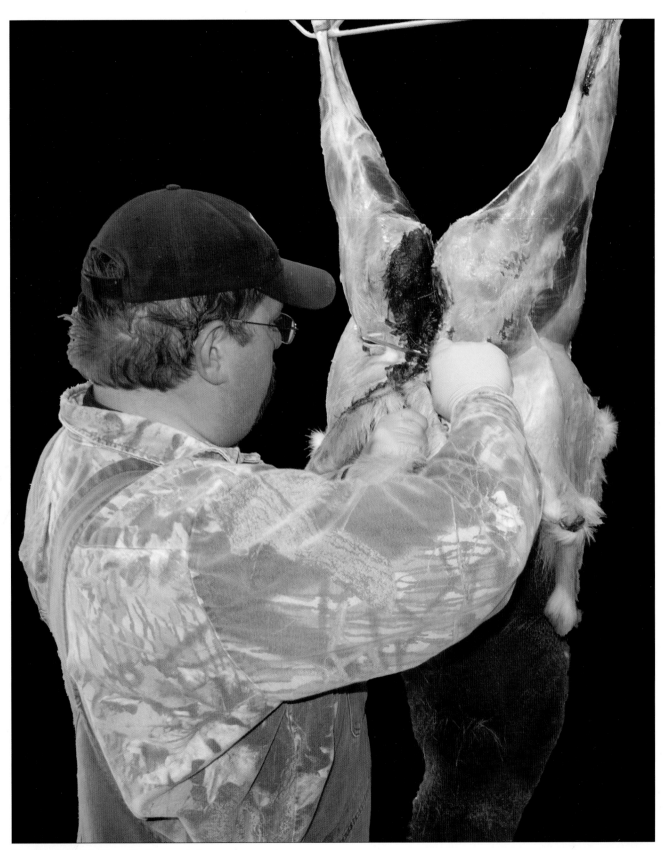

Carefully cut between the vertebrae.

CONSIDER CWD

If you're concerned about CWD, this is one of the steps you may want to perform with a knife that you've reserved for this purpose. Then go back to using your regular skinning knife.

as you work through this area. You'll still need to do a little cutting here and there. But if you pull as you cut, you'll get a good sense of when you really need to cut and when you can just keep peeling.

Notice that the hide is softer and thinner along the inner side of the hindquarters; if you pull too hard, it could tear. If this happens a little bit, don't worry about it. Keep going until both

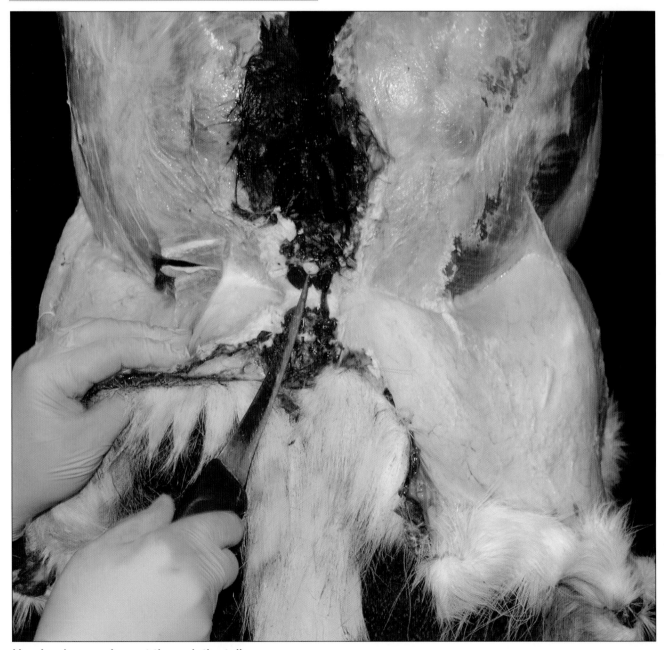

Here's where we've cut through the tail.

hindquarters are exposed all the way around.

Continue pulling the hide downward along either side of the tail. This is one area where hairs will come loose more easily. Don't panic if you see that happening. Later, we'll show you a few tricks for removing them. It will only take a few moments. Now, however, we've reached a small obstacle—the tail.

Skin Past the Tail

If you know how to do this, it's easy. We'll leave the tail attached to the skin, and carefully cut it off under the skin.

You've already pulled the adjacent skin away from the hindquarters. Grab the tail near its base, and pull down hard. When you do, you'll see a few vertebrae at the base of the tail. While

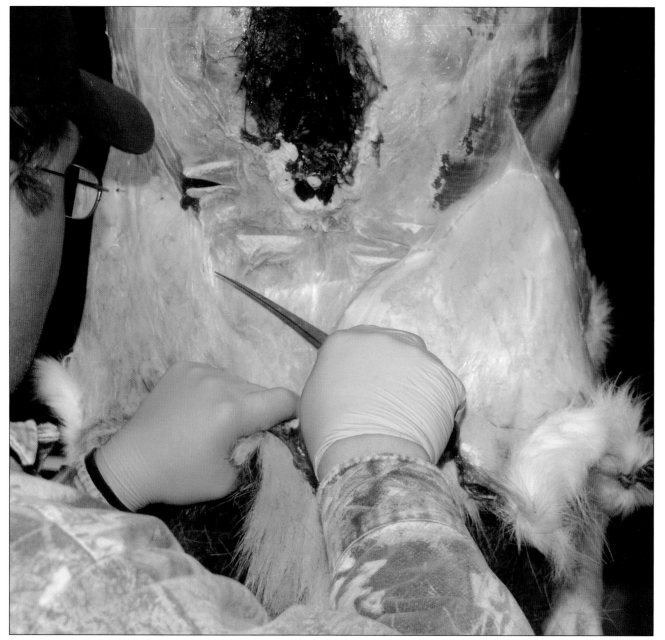

Continue pulling downward, cutting as you go.

still pulling downward on the tail with one hand, carefully cut between the vertebrae.

As you do, you'll feel the tail release. It will come free with the skin and you'll be able to see the exposed surface of the last vertebra that stays with the carcass. Now begin skinning downward along the abdomen and rib cage.

Skin the Abdomen and Rib Cage

Now you'll be able to really make some progress. On some deer you'll be able to peel the abdomen and the rib cage with very little cutting. Other deer, however, will still require a fair amount of cutting—especially if the meat is cold or if it's a tough old buck. Every deer is different.

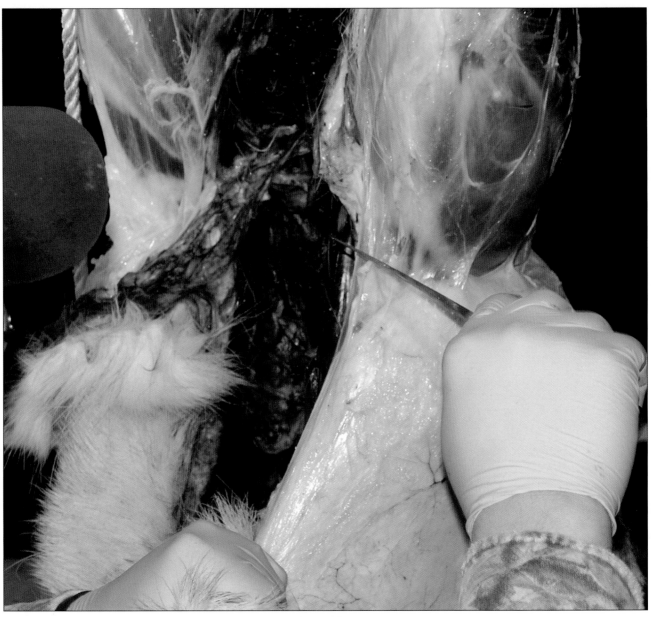

Turn the carcass around and begin skinning the other side.

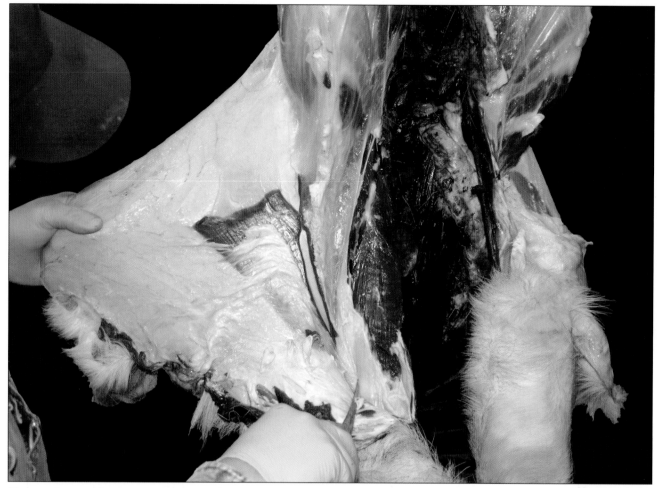

Now we're making some progress. In most cases, you'll be able to just keep pulling.

During this sequence, we've shown pictures from two different deer. On one deer, there's only a small amount of subcutaneous fat still attached to the inside of the hide. On the other, there's also a little bit of meat still adhering to the hide. Don't worry if that happens; these scraps will only add up to a few ounces of meat.

Before you go too far down the back, turn the carcass around and begin skinning from the cut you made during field dressing. As you be-

WHAT ABOUT THOSE FRONT LEGS?

If you haven't already skinned the front legs, do so before continuing. You'll find step-by-step instructions earlier in this chapter.

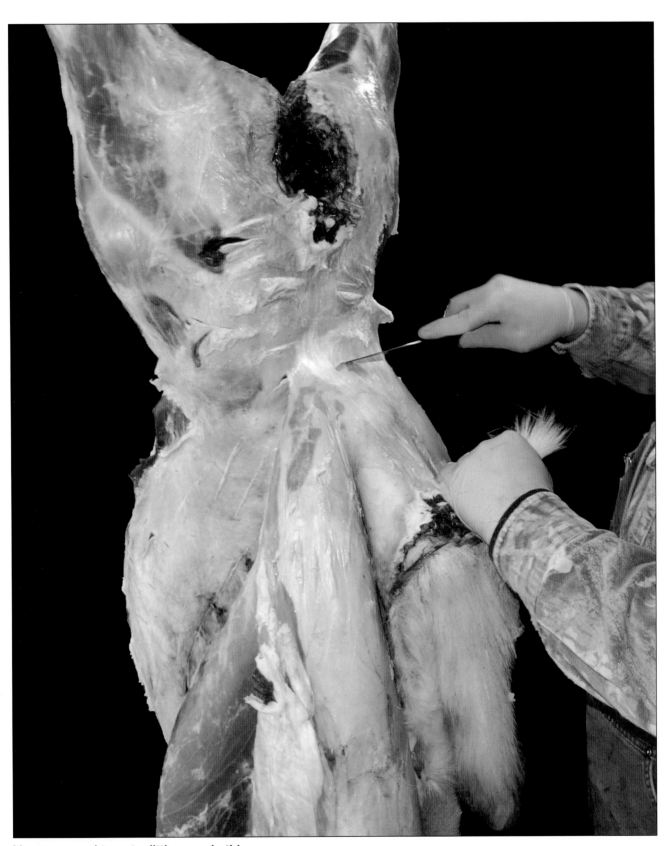

You may need to cut a little more in this area.

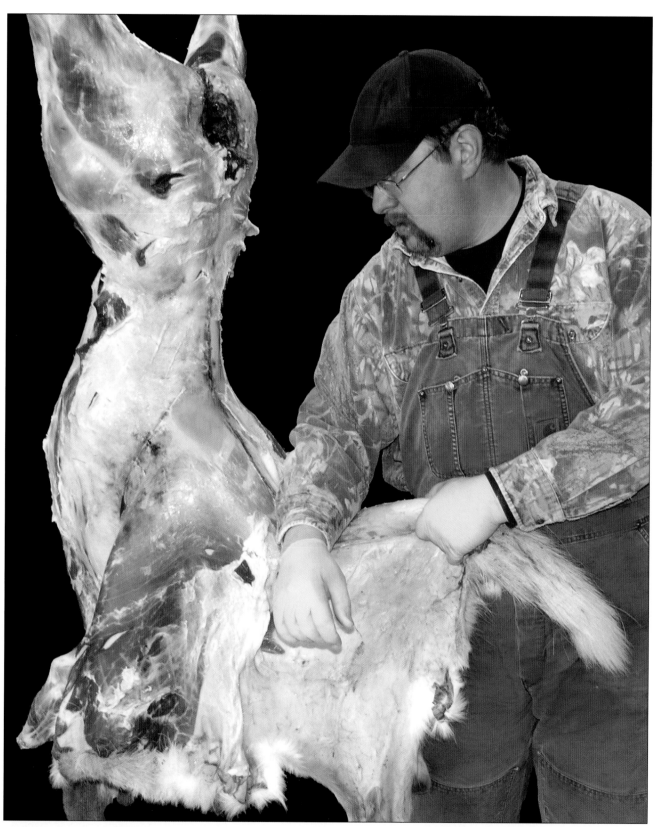

Now you can put down your knife and start peeling. Notice how Eric is pulling on the tail with his left hand while leaning into the skin with his right elbow.

gin trimming away from this edge, make small, careful cuts. This area will be dried out and hanging loose. You won't have much to push against and it's a little tricky getting started. Once you do, however, things get a lot easier.

Keep going along the abdomen and down the rib cage. Continue all the way to the front legs. Then do the same on the other side.

By now you've freed a large flap of skin along either side of the carcass. For now, however, don't cut all the way around the other side. Leave a six-to twelve inch strip attached along the backbone. (This width doesn't have to be precise, and it will depend in part on the size of your deer.)

Next it's time to take care of that remaining strip. Turn the carcass around so the back is facing you. On some deer, you may need to cut a little more in the area just past the hindquarters.

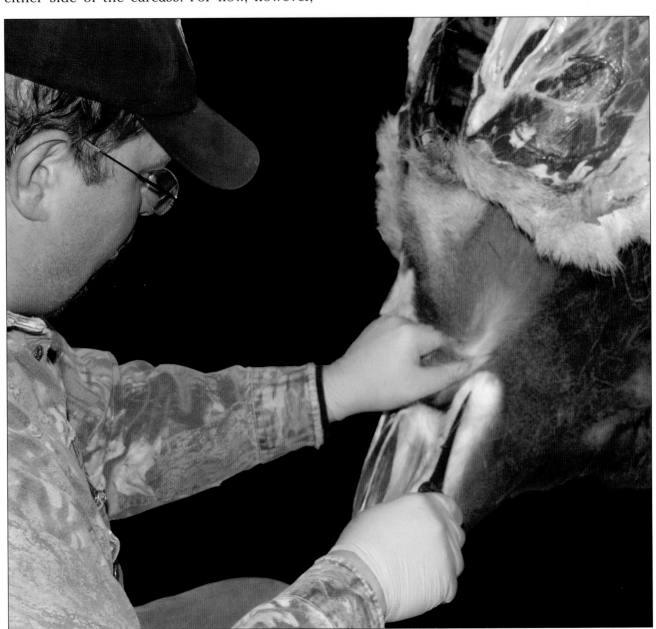

Extend the cuts you made along the back of the front legs.

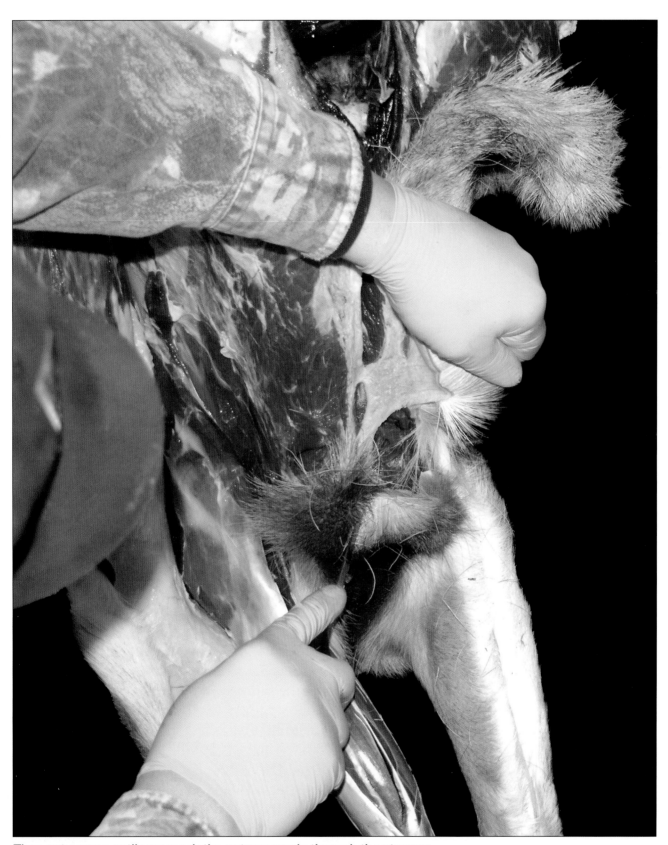

Then cut across until you reach the cut you made through the sternum.

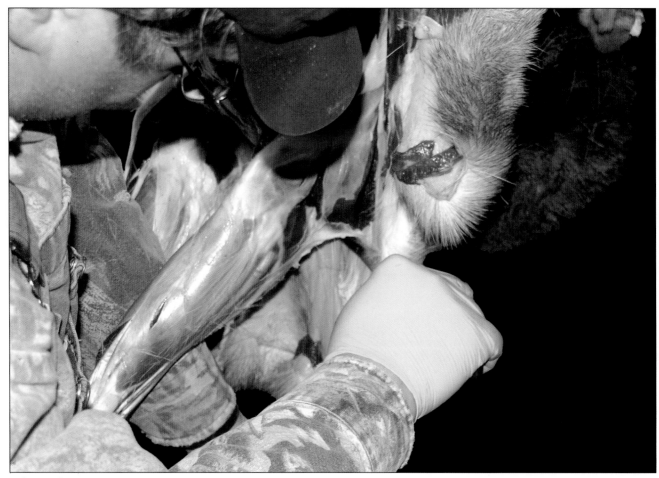

This area is especially challenging.

Now you can put your arm into it and really pull. On most deer you'll make easy progress during this step.

You may still need to do a little trimming with your knife now and then. If you're lucky, you'll be able to just pull all the way to the shoulders.

Skin Around the Shoulders

You just completed what's probably the easiest part of the skinning process. This next part, however, will go a little slower—especially when you're trimming around that awkward "armpit" area.

All that remains is to skin around the shoulders and skin the neck. If you shot a trophy buck that you'll to take to the taxidermist, STOP.

Follow the instructions in Chapter 15: Saving Antlers and Caping Your Trophy. If this deer's just for eating, continue skinning around the shoulders.

If you opened the deer's sternum during field-dressing, continue until you reach the central cut you made back then. If you haven't yet opened the sternum, that's okay. Instead, just slit the skin downward along the sternum. Continue until you reach a point midway between the front legs.

Once that's done, it's back to skinning. First, extend the cuts you made along the back of the front legs. Then, where the white "armpit" hair meets the brown side of the rib cage, cut across until you reach the cut you made through the sternum.

Consider CWD

If you're concerned about CWD, you may have decided to skin your deer with the head on. Just cut the hide free once you're most of the way down the neck. You can leave the head on the carcass as you're butchering.

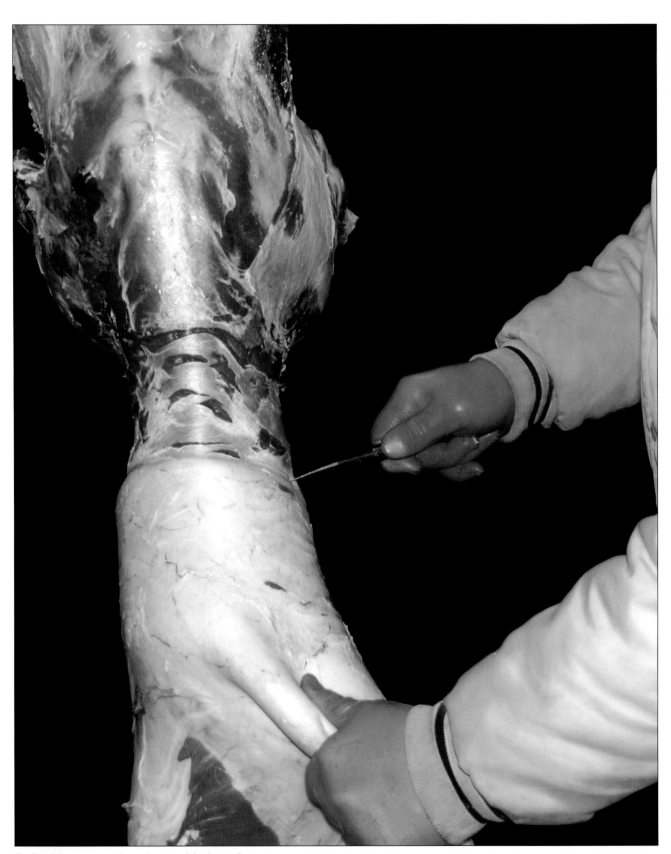

Pull with one hand and cut with the other.

Next, trim around the neck and the top of the shoulders. Then finish skinning that awkward area between the front legs. Be patient, keep your knife sharp, and carefully work your way past this area. This skin hangs on tight, it's thin and tears easily. Take your time.

This is another area where you'll encounter some loose hairs; don't worry if some get on the meat. In a moment, we'll tell you easy ways to remove them.

Now you're past the shoulders. All that's left is to skin the neck.

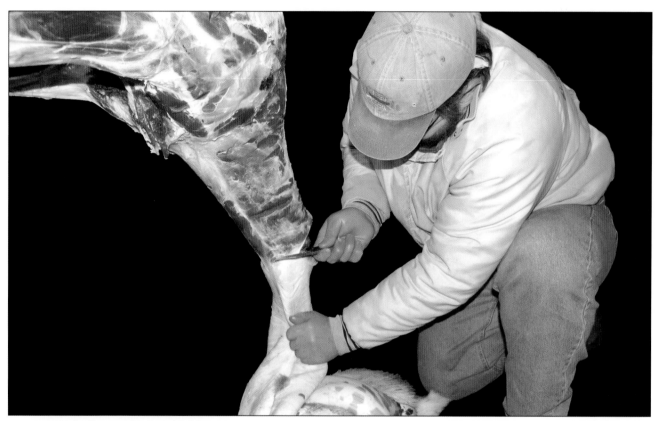

A few more slices and you're done.

Lay the skin out on the ground, fur-side down.

Fold one side toward the middle…

… and then the other.

Start rolling at the neck.

Finish with the tail.

Skin the Neck

The hide over a deer's neck is usually pretty well attached. Plan on doing a lot of cutting and not very much pulling and peeling. That's especially true for a large, rutting buck, where you could be cutting every inch of the way.

The best technique is to gently pull downward while using light, sweeping cuts that follow the contour of the neck. Don't worry if a few scraps of meat stay with the hide, especially at the end.

Keep skinning and pulling all the way to the end. A few more slices and you're done.

Save the Hide

A few hundred years ago, deer hides went for a dollar apiece. That's where the expression "a buck" came from. Unfortunately, prices have not kept pace with inflation. Today our local feed mill buys deer hides for three dollars. So keep your day job and don't sweat it if the hide comes off in tatters the first few times.

Eventually, though, you may want to save a few hides and try tanning them yourself. You

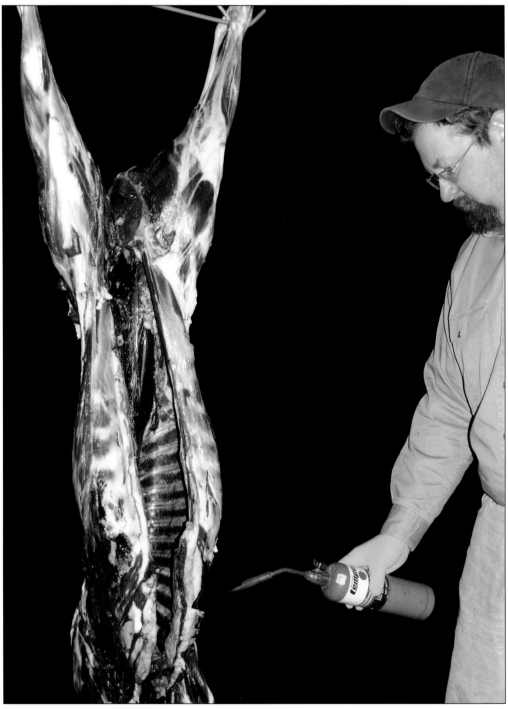

Remove hairs with a blowtorch.

Remove hairs with a damp paper towel.

can also pay to have them tanned commercially; look for ads in the back of hunting magazines.

To preserve the hide, coat the inner side with lots of salt. This draws out the moisture so the hide won't become soggy and easily torn.

If you didn't slit the neck during skinning, the neck portion of the hide will be inside-out. After salting it down, reach in to turn it right side-out. Then carefully fold it over so the inner layers are together and the fur side is out. Finally, roll it into a bundle, starting at the neck and finishing at the tail.

Removing Those Pesky Hairs

Congratulations! You finished skinning your deer.

There's just one detail remaining—those pesky hairs. Now might be a good time to remove them, rather than later at the dinner table. Here are two ways to do it.

First, there's the blowtorch method. This method is quick and easy, especially if there are just a few hairs. In the fall and winter, deer have hollow hairs that provide tremendous insulation. These burn off with a satisfying pop. But don't go having too much fun with this. Keep your torch moving and don't precook your venison.

The second method is not nearly as much fun. It does, however, work better if there are lots of hairs sticking to the carcass. Just dab them away with a damp rag or a piece of paper towel. Occasionally switch to a fresh piece of towel, dip it in a bowl of warm water, and dab away.

Ideally, avoid getting those hairs on your venison in the first place. Sometimes that's difficult. With either of these techniques, it will only take a minute or two to remove them.

Now might be a good time to take a break...

Wait a minute. What time is it getting to be?

You're done skinning and it's time to begin butchering. If you'd like to postpone the rest of the job until tomorrow, now might be a good time to stop.

Depending on the temperature and how long your deer has already been hanging, it might even be a good idea to let the carcass cool so the meat can firm up and be easier to cut. Make sure, however, that you'll be able to keep the carcass from either freezing or getting too warm.

It's your call. If you like, take a break.

Then, whenever you're ready, it's time to open the butcher shop.

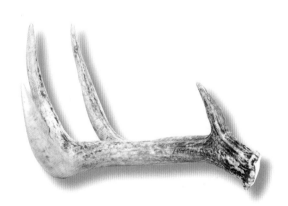

CHAPTER 8

Butchering The Shoulder Cuts

You finished skinning your deer. Now it's time to begin butchering.

The shoulders are an easy, no-pressure way to get started. Because these cuts tend to be a little tougher, you'll cut most of this meat into small pieces for burger or stew. You may decide to use some of it for shoulder roasts; just remember that they'll need a little more cooking. We usually mark these packages "roasts for slow cooker."

The chunks reserved for burger and stew can be any size or shape. As you work, accumulate them in a bowl set aside for this purpose. (We call this our "burger bucket.") Later, you can grind them into hamburger or cut them into stew-sized chunks.

Remove the Front Leg

This step will be easier than you might think. You won't need to cut through any bones, and you won't even need to precisely locate a joint where you can separate the leg. That's because a deer's front leg is only attached by muscle and connective tissue.

To remove the front leg, first pull it outward and away from the rib cage. When you do, you'll be able to see right where your knife should go. Keep a firm grip on the lower part of the leg; the first time you do this, you'll be surprised at how quickly and easily it comes free.

Begin slicing parallel to the rib cage. Keep pull-

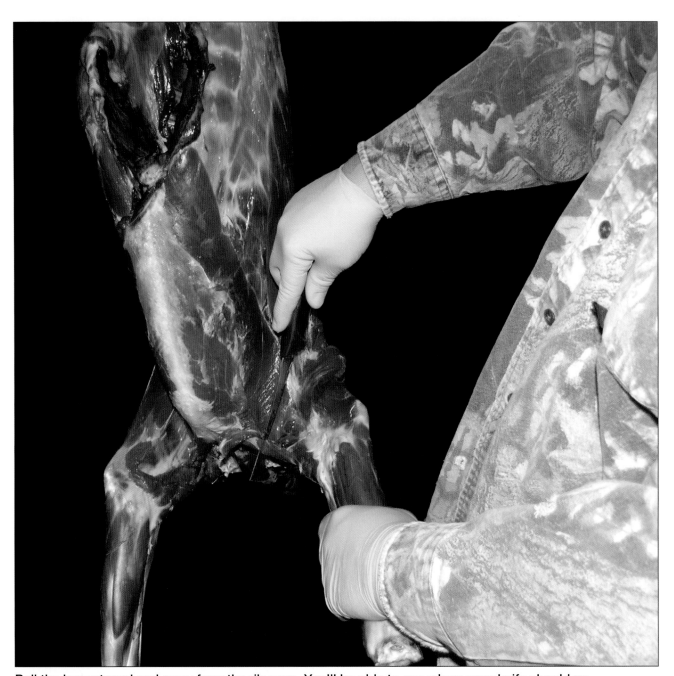

Pull the leg outward and away from the rib cage. You'll be able to see where your knife should go.

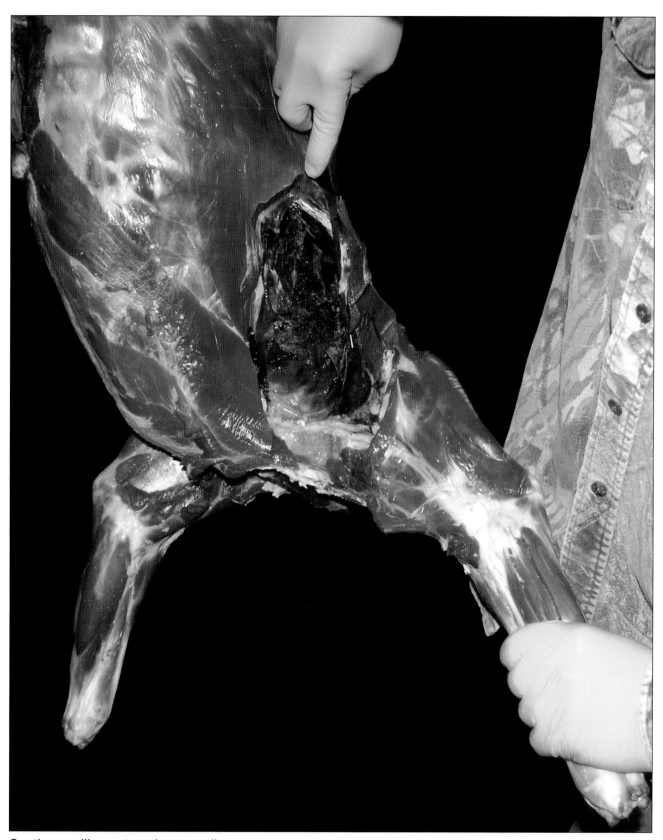

Continue pulling outward as you slice.

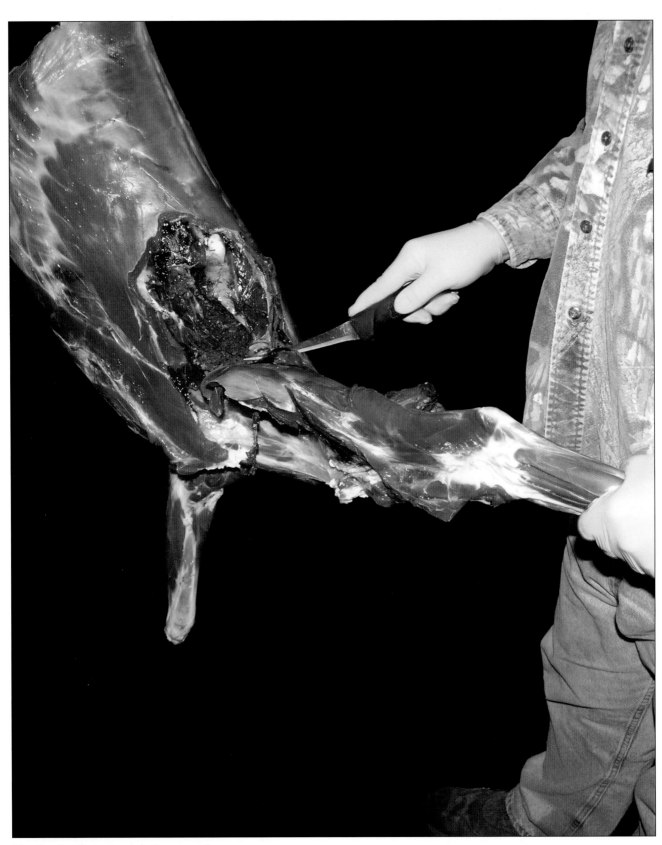

The leg is almost ready to come free.

Trim away any bloodshot meat.

Beware of jagged bone fragments
or pieces of bullet jacket.

Is there lead in your venison?

Because early studies addressing this question were often based on questionable methodologies and a small number of samples, their results were easily dismissed. More recent studies, however, confirm that there may indeed be reason for concern. Small bullet fragments sometimes travel well beyond the wound channel and well outside the area that's visibly bloodshot.

The problem is most likely to occur when hunters combine high-velocity calibers with rapidly expanding bullets. It's less likely with shotgun slugs, muzzleloader bullets, or heavy, slow-moving calibers.

If you're concerned about lead, here's how you can reduce the risk:

+ Consider using non-toxic loads made from copper or other metals. These premium loads offer controlled expansion and excellent penetration; they also hold together without fragmenting.

+ If you stick with conventional jacketed bullets that have a lead core, choose bullet types that promise controlled expansion and maximum weight retention.

+ Be especially careful to trim away all bloodshot meat. If the bullet has hit bone, trim away even more of the adjacent area.

+ Avoid shoulder shots. Instead, try for that classic broadside shot right behind the shoulder. The bullet won't hit anything more solid than ribs, will probably exit on the far side, and will leave behind far fewer fragments.

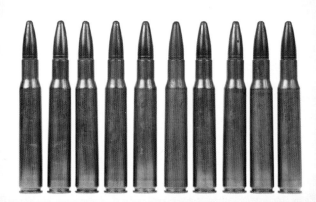

ing the front leg outward as you slice. When the knife goes past the inside of the shoulder blade, you're almost there. Cut through the remaining flap of muscle and the front leg will come free.

Next, take the front leg over to your table or workbench. If you have plenty of room on your bench, now might also be a good time to remove the other front leg. Or you can leave it on until you're done cutting up the first leg.

Even the first time, this step will probably take less time to complete than it took to read about it.

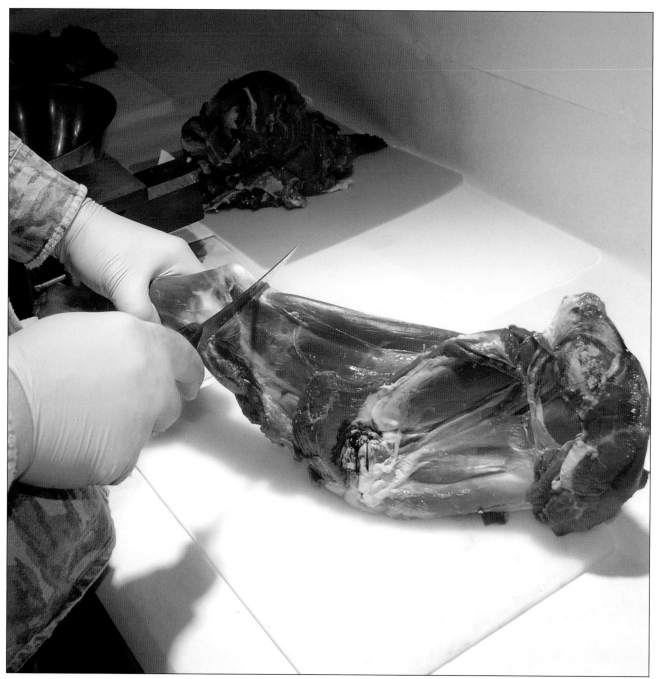

Begin your cut about an inch above the joint.

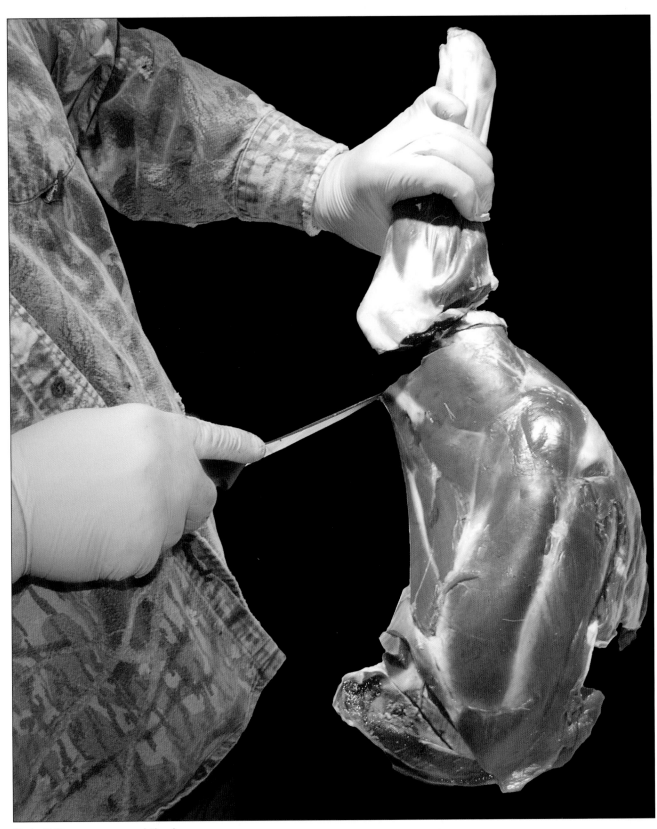

Cut all the way around the leg.

Trim Away Any Bloodshot Meat

If you've aimed for the shoulder or the heart-lung area, you could encounter some bloodshot meat during this step. You'll see an area with a reddish, jelly-like appearance. Trim this away and discard it.

As you do, be careful of jagged edges where bones have been damaged by your bullet or arrow. There could also be a few fragments of metal from the bullet or its jacket; sometimes these can be sharp, too.

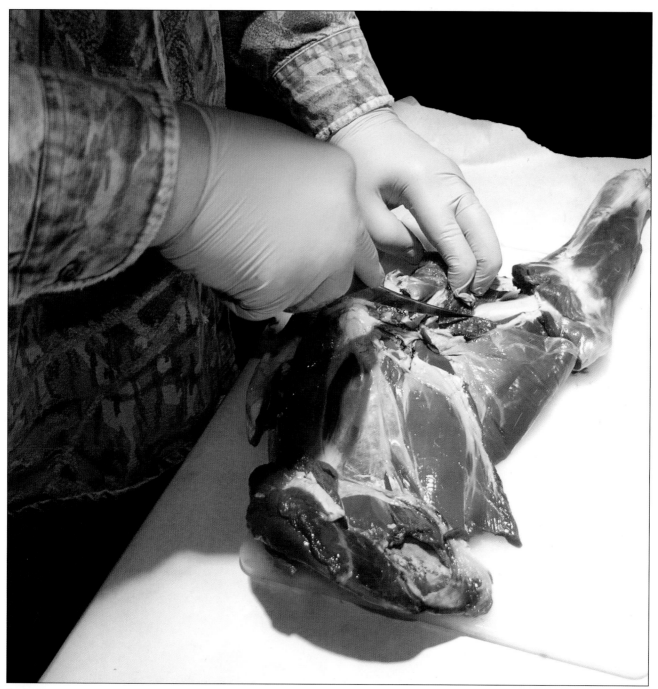

Cut along the length of this bone.

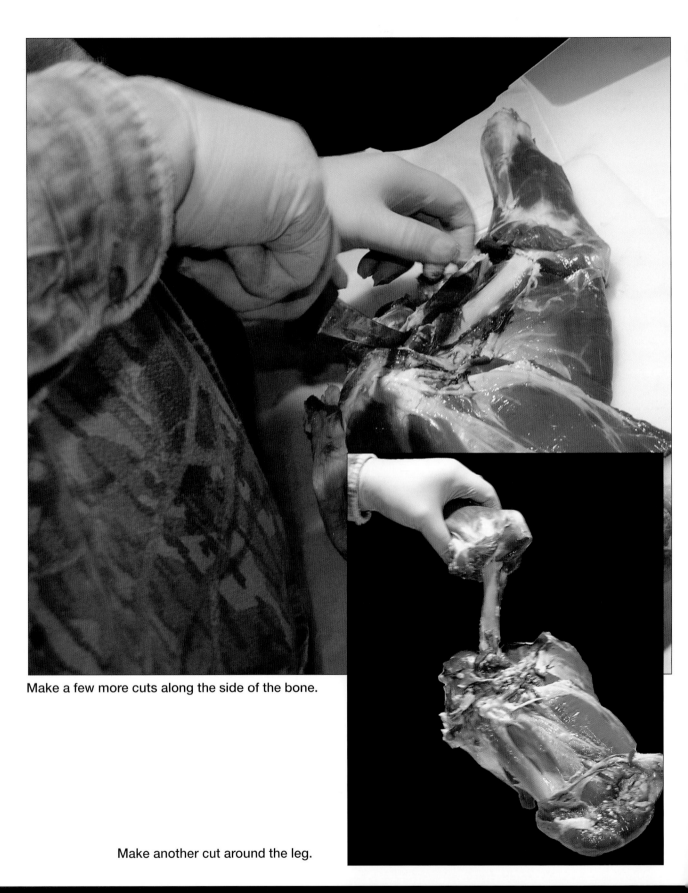

Make a few more cuts along the side of the bone.

Make another cut around the leg.

Cut along the length of this ridge.

Fillet along surface of the scapula.

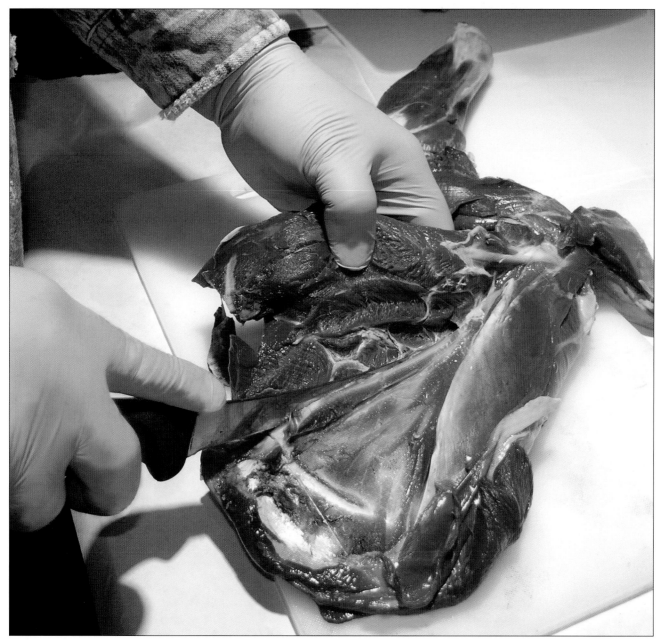

Make a few more cuts on this side...

Debone the Middle Portion of the Front Leg

Hold the front leg as shown in the photo. Begin your cut about an inch above the joint. Cut all the way down to the bone, but stop when your knife reaches the bone. Continue to cut all the way around the leg. Let your knife ride gently against the bone; extra pressure will only dull your knife.

Lay the leg down with the inside facing up.

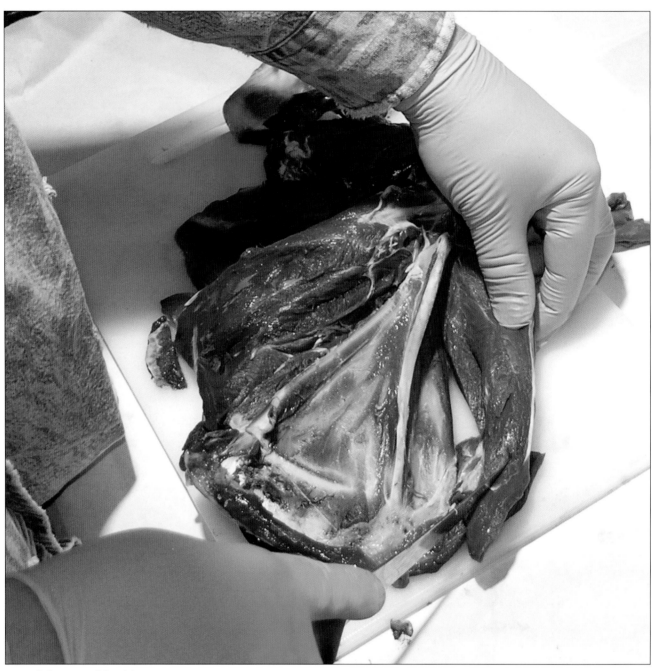

...and then on this side.

Next, cut along the length of the leg, starting at the point where you just cut around the leg. There's a bone just below the surface; make a slit just above it.

As you do, you'll uncover the bone. With a few additional cuts along the side of the bone, the meat will come free fairly easily.

Just below the shoulder, make another cut around the leg. You have now freed this entire piece from the middle portion of the front leg.

A quick lesson in deer anatomy. This is the deer's front right leg, positioned just as it was when it was still on the deer.

This piece may still need some extra trimming. You can do that now or debone another piece and trim them both at the same time.

Debone the Upper Portion of the Front Leg

Flip the leg over so the outside is facing up. Once again, you'll see a bone that's just under the surface. It's a ridge on the shoulder bone. Cut along the length of that bone.

Next, fillet downward along the inside of this bone. Then run your knife horizontally along the large, flat surface. This is the deer's shoulder blade, also known as the scapula.

On either side of the scapula, make a few more cuts—first on one side and then on the other. You'll probably also need to cut free a few more bits here and there. Before you know it, you'll have removed a large chunk of meat from the outside of the shoulder bone.

Good job. Before we continue, let's pause for a quick lesson in deer anatomy. On page 161, you can see the bone structure of the deer's right front leg, positioned just as it was when it was still on the deer.

Why the Shank May Not Be Worth Saving

In that last photo you may have noticed some meat still attached to the lower leg—but not

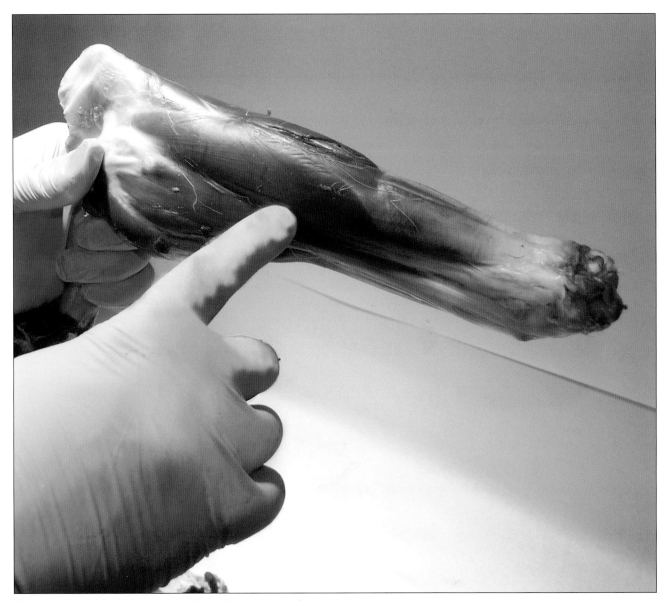

The shanks include lots of tendons, but not much meat.

much. Depending on the size of the deer, there's probably only about half a pound of shank meat on each leg. You'll also find lots of tendons and connective tissue.

Although we're fairly frugal, we don't always save the shanks. But if you like, give them a try. If nothing else, they work great for soup stock.

Shoulder Roasts, Stew Meat, Burgers, and Sausage

In this picture, you can see the chunks of meat we've just removed from the front leg. They're positioned just as they were when they were on the bone. Next, we'll convert these pieces into roasts, stew meat, burger and sausage.

You could slice nearly all these pieces up and tie them into roast-sized chunks. Usually, however, we just make roasts out of the largest muscle groups in the shoulder.

The meat from one front leg.

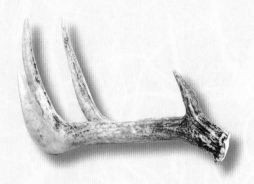

THE TAO OF DEER DISASSEMBLY

Back in about the third century B.C., Chuang Tzu described the mindset of a skillful butcher. His words capture perfectly the essence of deer disassembly:

"…Trusting in the Tao, I send my knife slicing through cavernous crevices; it touches neither joint nor bone. A good cook needs a new knife once a year; he chops. A poor cook needs a new knife once a month; he hacks. I've used this same knife nineteen years. It has butchered a thousand oxen, and it's still like new.

…There are spaces in the joints; a sharp, thin blade can slide right through. When I get to a more difficult joint, I pause to consider it. Then I move my knife slowly and carefully, and bam! The part falls away, landing like a clod of earth."

However you decide to use these cuts, you'll need to trim away some fat, gristle and connective tissue. Be especially careful when you trim away the lymph nodes; they're located on the inside of the shoulder, up in the "armpit" area. Trim them away along the edges, being careful to not puncture them.

In the picture on page 166, we're trimming some fat, connective tissue and "silverskin" from the outside of the roast. Most of this tissue softens and breaks down during cooking, but we like to trim away as much as possible.

Butcher the Other Front Leg, and Get Ready for Steaks

Next, follow these same steps to butcher the other front leg. Then you'll be ready for the tenderloins and backstrap.

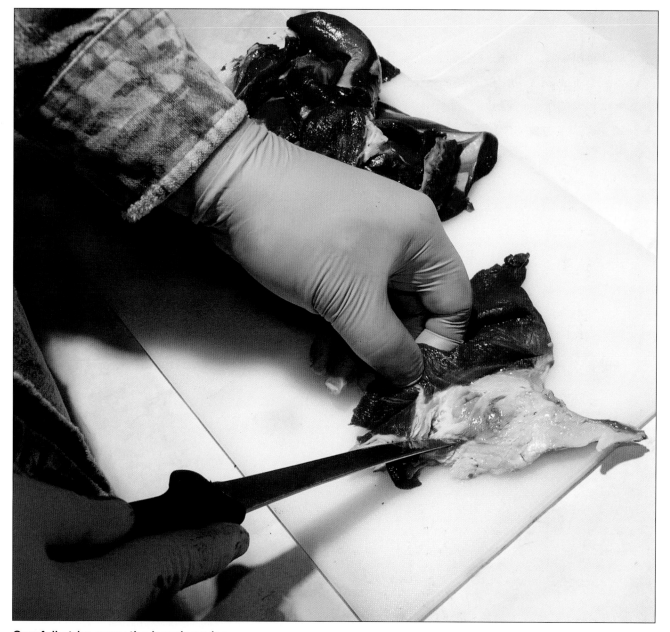

Carefully trim away the lymph nodes.

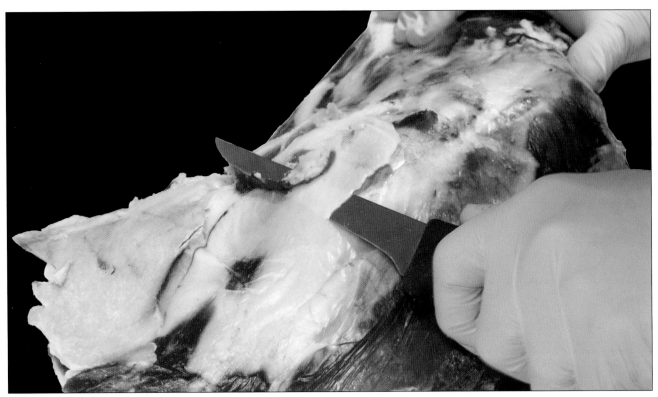

Trimming the outside of a shoulder roast.

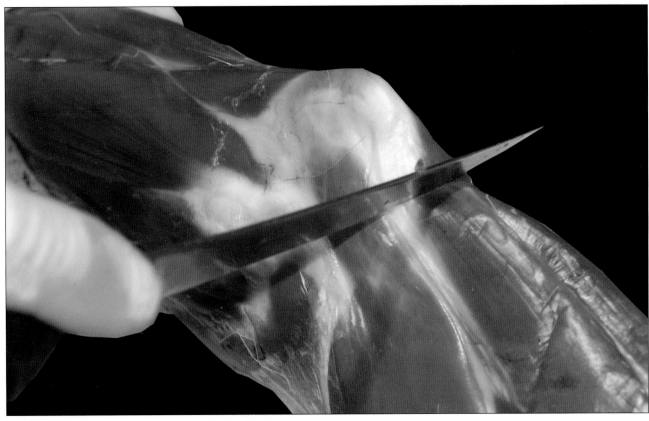

Now do the other front leg.

CHAPTER 9
Removing the Tenderloins and Backstraps

In the tamer world of beef, tenderloins would correspond to filet mignon; backstraps would correspond to T-bone steaks, but without the annoying T-bone. Both will be tender, boneless cuts that are fairly easy to butcher.

Give Yourself Some Maneuvering Room

Let's start with the tenderloins. They're inside the body cavity, just forward of the hindquarters. (Some hunters like to remove them during field-dressing; we'll assume you've waited until now.) To make the job easier, trim away the abdominal muscles along either side. For now, fold them over the rib cage to get them out of the way.

Later we'll remove these pieces and save them for hamburger. But they're relatively thin; if they dried out, or if it's a small deer, they may not be worth saving.

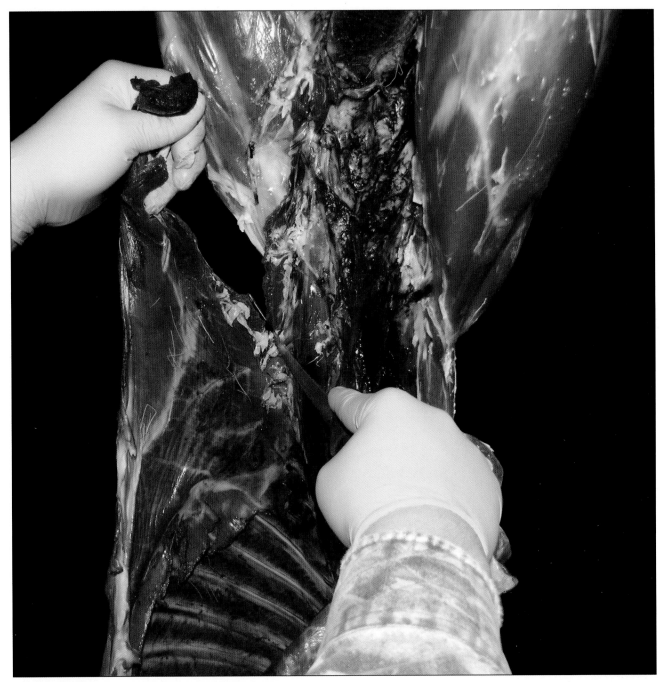

Trim the flanks away to give yourself more maneuvering room.

In these photos, however, you'll see meat that looks fresh and tasty enough so it wouldn't seem out of place in your supermarket's meat department—maybe marked as extra-lean venison bacon. As a matter of fact, this is exactly the part of a pig that gets turned into bacon. On a deer, however, these cuts are much thinner and leaner.

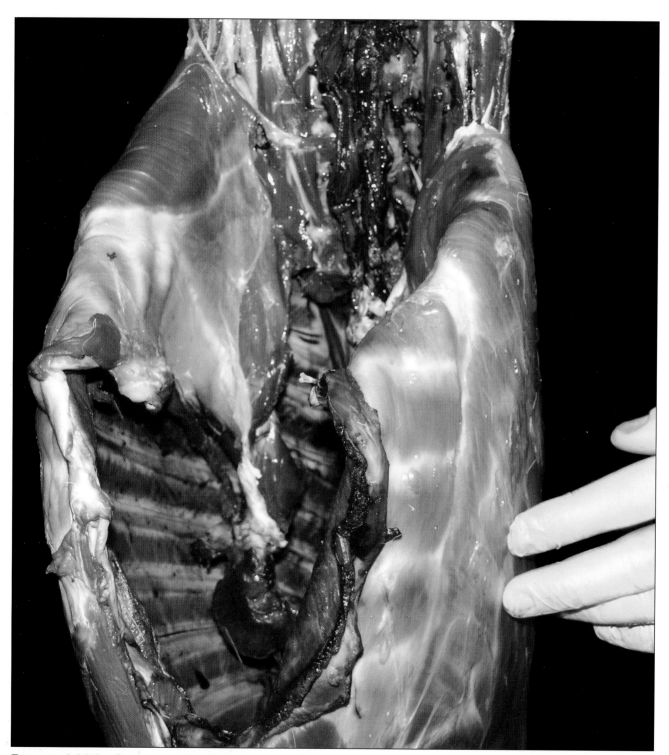

For now, fold the flanks over the rib cage.

Uncover the Tenderloins

Next, you may need to uncover the tenderloins by trimming away some fat and connective tissue. This is another step where every deer will be different. Some will have more fat than others, or they'll have it in different places. In this photo we've had to cut and peel away some fat and connective tissue to uncover the tenderloins.

Remove the Tenderloins

Once you've uncovered the tenderloins, you can get a better idea of where they're positioned by sliding your fingers behind them; they're only attached at either end.

Next, cut the tenderloins free at the end closest to the hindquarters. Then work them free with your fingers while peeling them out and downward. You may need to make a few cuts

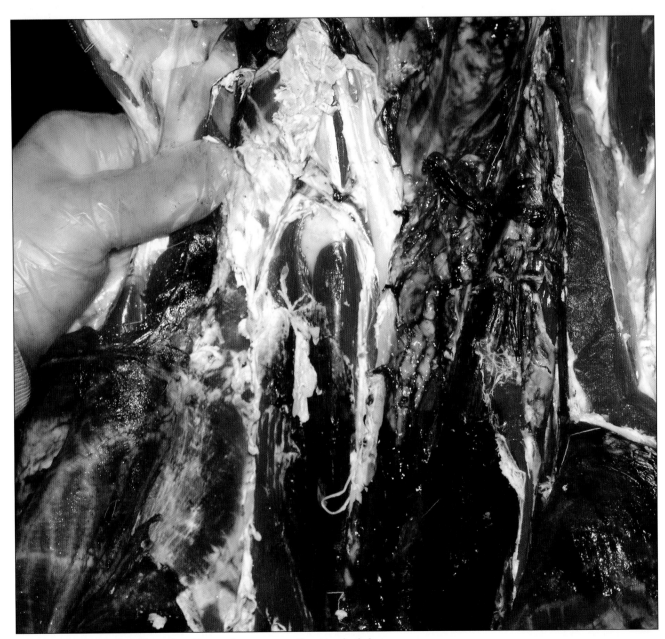

Trim away fat and connective tissue to uncover the tenderloins.

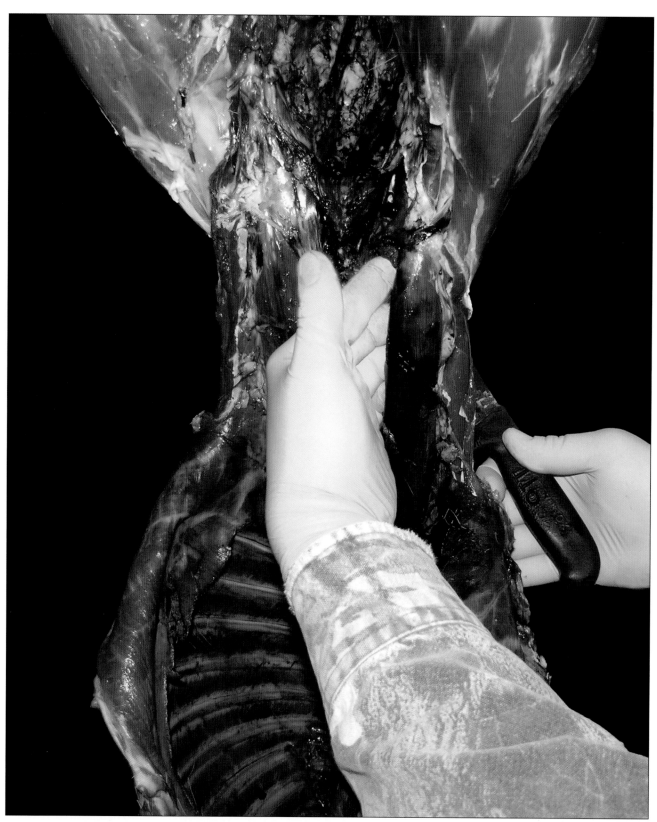

Slip your fingers behind the tenderloin to get a better idea of where the ends are located.

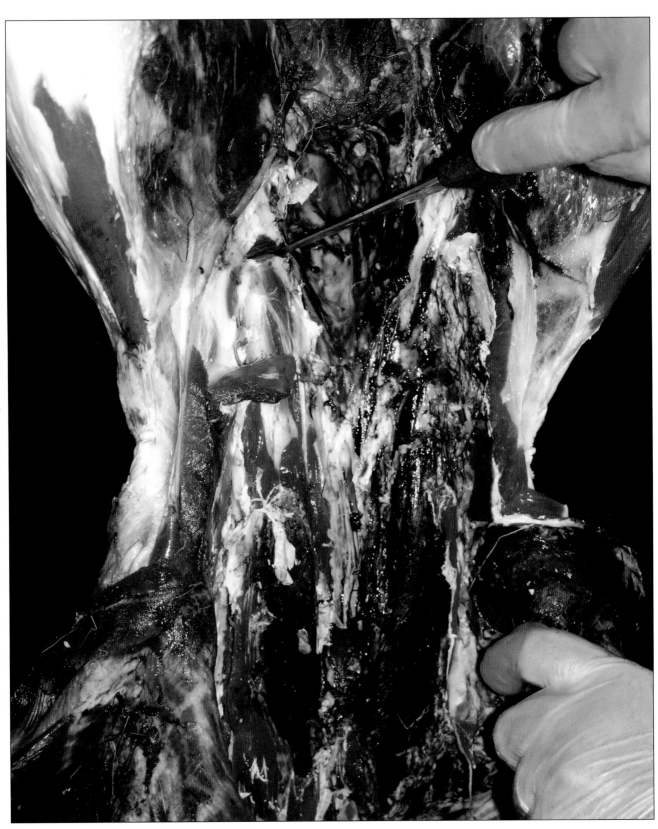

Cut this end free first.

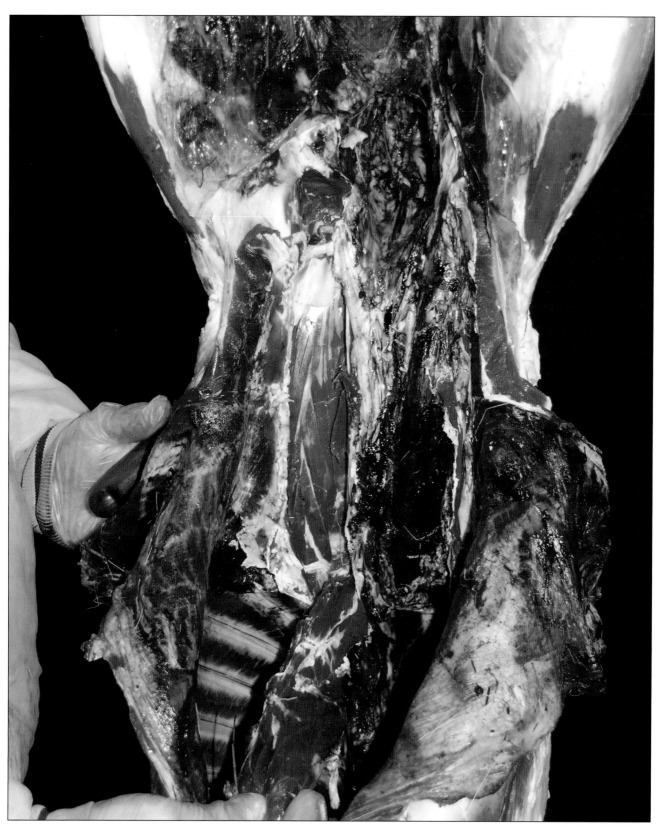

Remove the tenderloins by peeling outward.

along the way. Usually, however, they'll peel right out. Then cut them free at the bottom.

The tenderloins may come out looking a little ragged; that's okay. Once they're out you can square off the ends and trim away any dried areas. Then slice the remaining portion across the grain. You'll end up with tender "medallions" perfect for a stir-fry recipe. Or, more tradition- ally, tenderloins fried with butter and onions are a popular menu item at many deer camps.

Locate the Backstraps and Make Your Initial Cut

Next, it's time to remove the backstraps. They're large strips of meat along either side of the backbone. Once you remove them you'll slice them into steaks.

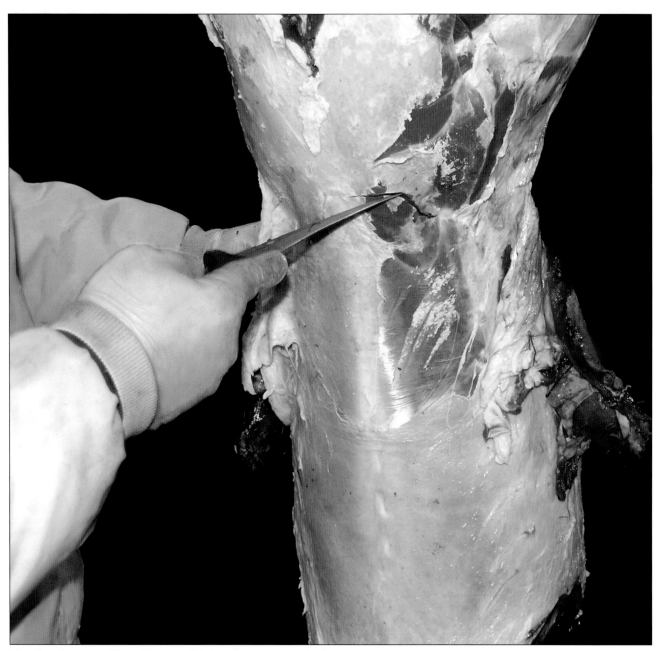

Here's where you'll make your first cut to remove the backstraps.

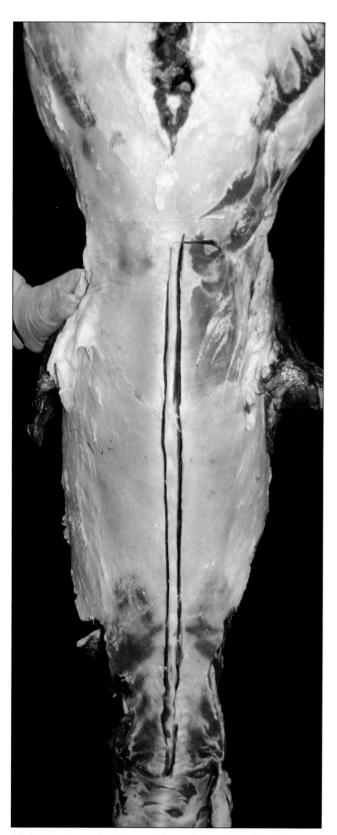

Make these cuts along either side of the backbone.

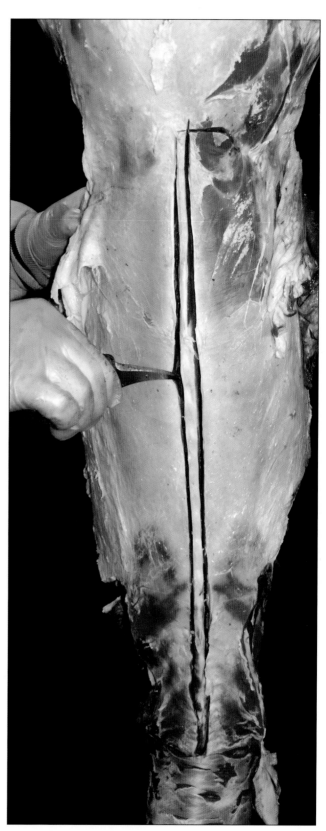

You may want to make a second pass.

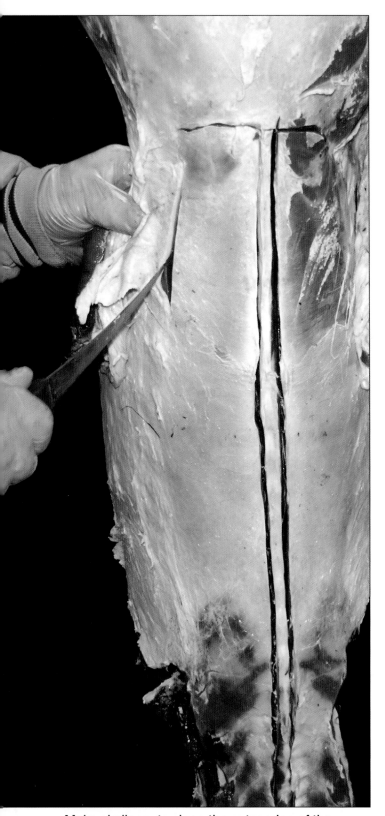

Make similar cuts along the outer edge of the backstrap.

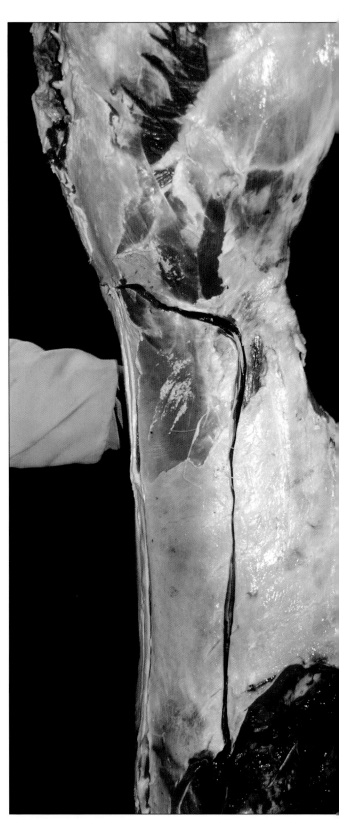

Extend these cuts all the way down to where the shoulder was.

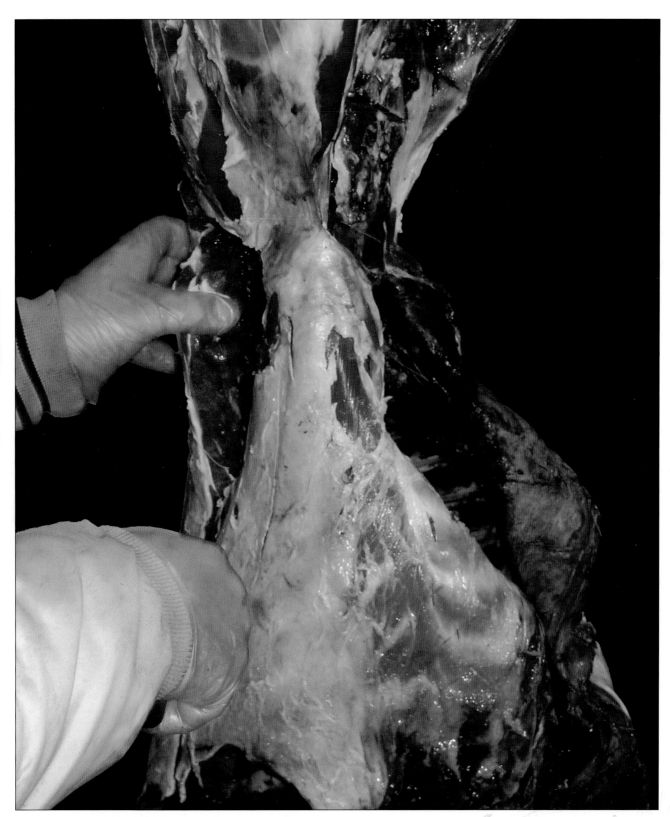

Now fillet inward from the outer cut.

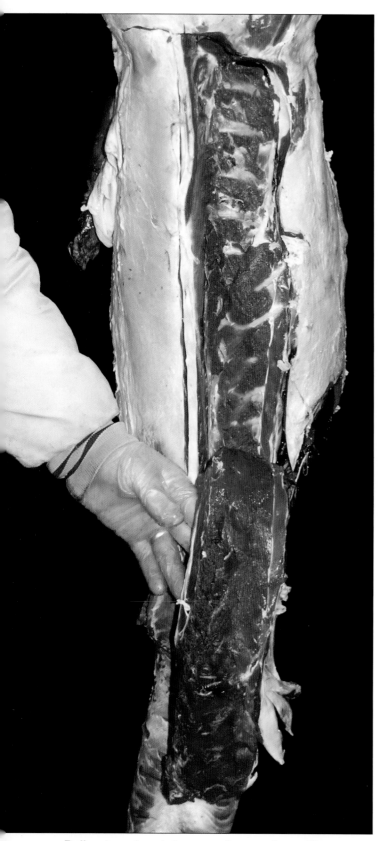

Pull outward and downward as you're cutting.

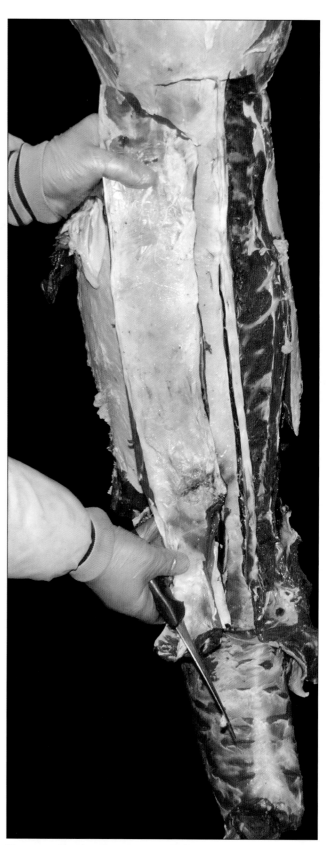

Remove the backstrap carefully.

Begin with cuts along the rear of the back-straps, just ahead of the hindquarters. Then make a cut along either side of the spinal column, but not through it. Leave the spinal column intact for now.

To find your starting point more precisely, look about three or four inches down from the tail. Locate the first vertebra forward from the hip. You'll be able to feel two bony projections on either side of it. Just below there, make a horizontal cut, with a diagonal corner at the outside.

Make Additional Cuts Around the Backstraps

Next, cut along the inside of the backstrap, parallel and immediately adjacent to the backbone. Continue downward until you reach a point about even with where the shoulders were. Then make a similar cut on the other side of the backbone.

Once you've made these cuts, you may want to run your knife up and down them a few more times to make sure they go all the way down to the bone. Do this carefully; deepen the cuts without dulling the edge of your knife against the bone.

Next, make similar cuts along the outer edge of the backstrap. When you begin at the hindquarters, make a deep cut parallel to the first one. Then, as you extend this cut all the way to where the shoulder was, you'll be cutting along the edge of what's going to be a much thinner slice of meat. As you get closer to the shoulder area, carefully slide your knife along the curvature of the rib cage.

Although this outer cut will meet up with the inner one along the backbone, the backstraps

It's just like filleting a fish.

Next, slice the backstraps into steaks.

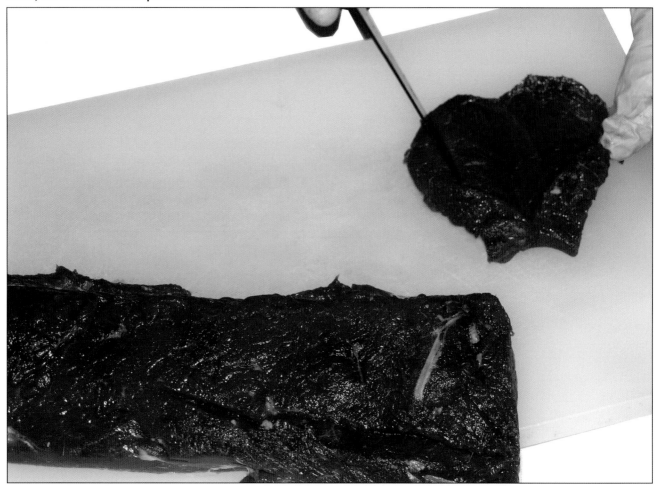

Making "butterfly" steaks.

will still be attached by bits of meat that you haven't cut through completely.

Remove the Backstraps

During this step, pull and peel the backstrap out and downward. You'll need to make a few more cuts to loosen the top corners, and you may even need to make a few cuts as you're peeling. But once you get started, you can fold the backstrap out and let gravity help you. When you get to the bottom, cut the backstrap loose and lift it free.

If you're butchering a large deer, you'll need to lift the backstrap with both hands. Whatever you do, don't drop it. It's best cut of prime venison on the entire deer.

Now follow these same steps to remove the other backstrap.

Again, don't panic if this doesn't go perfectly. If a few scraps of prime backstrap are still attached here and there, just trim them off and use them for burgers, stir-fries or fajitas. You'll still have plenty of steaks.

Trim the Backstraps and Slice Them Into Steaks

Lay the backstrap on the table. Then fillet the "silverskin" from the side of the backstrap. It's as easy as filleting a fish.

Next, slice these backstraps into steaks. The ragged end pieces can go into your "burger bucket." Or, since they're especially tender cuts, you may want to set them aside for stir-fries or fajitas.

No matter what size or shape these steaks are, they'll taste great. If you'd like larger steaks, use the "butterfly" method. Begin by slicing off a steak that's twice as thick as the dimension you want; if you'd like steaks an inch thick, slice off a slab that's two inches thick.

Then, very carefully, begin slicing this piece in half. Stop just before you get all the way through. Finally, open the "butterfly" and flatten it out into a steak that's half as thick but twice as large.

If you'd like something even larger for the grill, don't slice the backstraps into steaks at all. Just slice each one into two or three large chunks of boneless meat. Grill them slowly until the inside is pink, and they'll be delicious.

You've finished the tenderloins and backstraps. Next, we'll work on the ribs, brisket and neck. These cuts aren't as tender as the tenderloins and backstrap, but they're great for burger, sausage and stew.

CHAPTER 10

Butchering the Ribs, Brisket and Neck

If you just finished the backstraps, that was the fun part. In a few minutes, you removed two large pieces of prime, boneless venison. A few minutes more and you had them all carved up into steaks.

Next, however, you'll work on some cuts that are a little more work. You'll trim carefully to free each piece, then trim some more to separate the meat from layers of fat or connective tissue. After a while, you may reach a point of diminishing returns. It just may not feel worthwhile to spend another half-hour for that last half-pound of meat.

One factor influencing these choices will be the deer itself. A small deer, for example, won't have a lot of meat on its neck. On a large, rutting buck, the neck alone might yield twenty pounds of burger, sausage or stew meat.

Trim Meat From the Flanks, Ribs and Brisket

Earlier, you partially freed a piece from either side of the abdomen. To keep it out of the way, you folded over against the back of the rib cage. Now, go ahead and trim this layer away from either side of the rib cage.

Starting at the rear of the rib cage, fillet this piece from the rib cage. As you do, pull outward and downward as you go. Continue all the way to the where the shoulders were. When you reach the front of the rib cage, this entire piece will be free.

Keep a firm grip when you get to that point. You'll still be filleting with one hand; and in your other hand you'll be holding one end of what's becoming a fairly large, heavy sheet of venison.

After trimming these flank pieces from both sides, you may want to do a little more trimming at the bench. You'll find layers of meat and fat, plus a small amount of connective tissue. Depending on the deer, there could be a fair amount of meat on these two pieces.

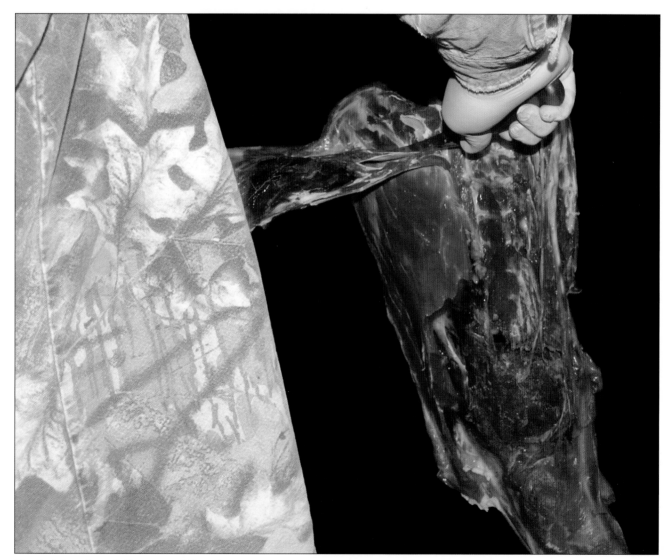

Begin trimming at the rear of the rib cage.

Continue along the outside of the rib cage.

Keep a firm grip when this piece is almost free.

Trim Meat From Between the Ribs

There won't be a lot of meat left on the ribs that you just uncovered. Even on a large deer it would probably total less than a pound. On the other hand, it will only take a minute or two to trim out these remaining slivers of meat.

If you'd like to try barbecued deer ribs, skip the previous steps and leave the outer "flank" layer attached to the ribs. But because deer are so lean, this dish usually turns out to be much drier and tougher than beef or pork ribs would be.

Nearly all of the remaining meat on the rib cage is right in between the ribs. It's a thin layer that's relatively dry and stringy. If you weren't able to clean inside the rib cage thoroughly after field-dressing, then you'll also need to trim away some dried blood.

For these reasons the meat between the ribs may not be worth salvaging on some deer. Generally, however, we like to trim out these strips and add them to the burger bucket.

Trim Meat From the Neck

Continue working on the neck while the remainder of the carcass is still hanging. Or, if the neck isn't at a comfortable working height, take part of the carcass down and work on it more over at the bench.

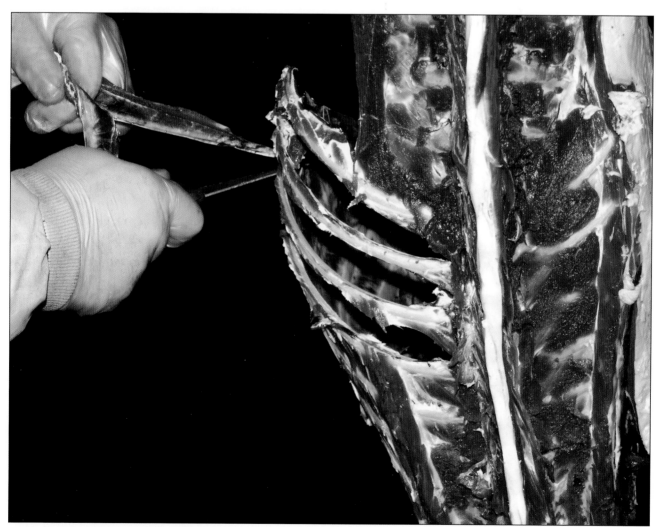

Trim meat from between the ribs.

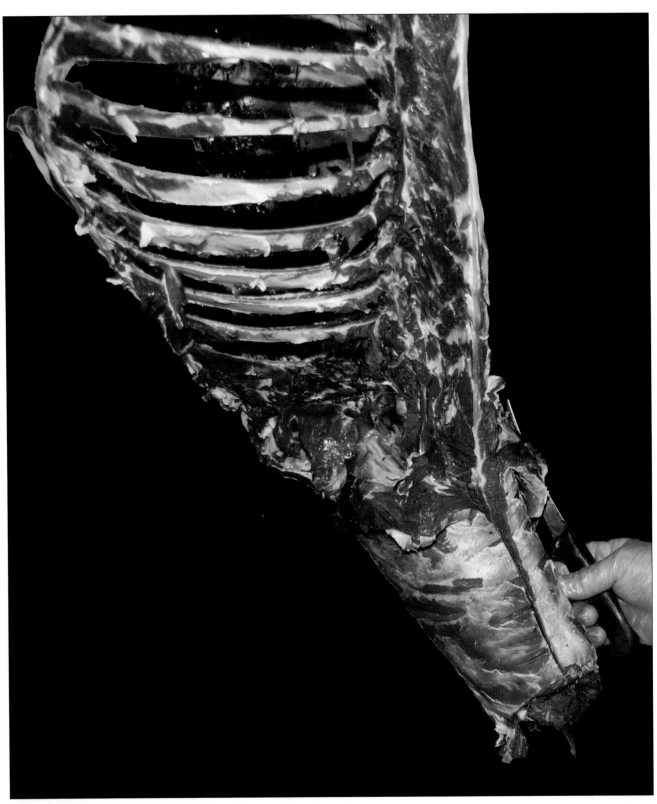

Cut along either side of the spine.

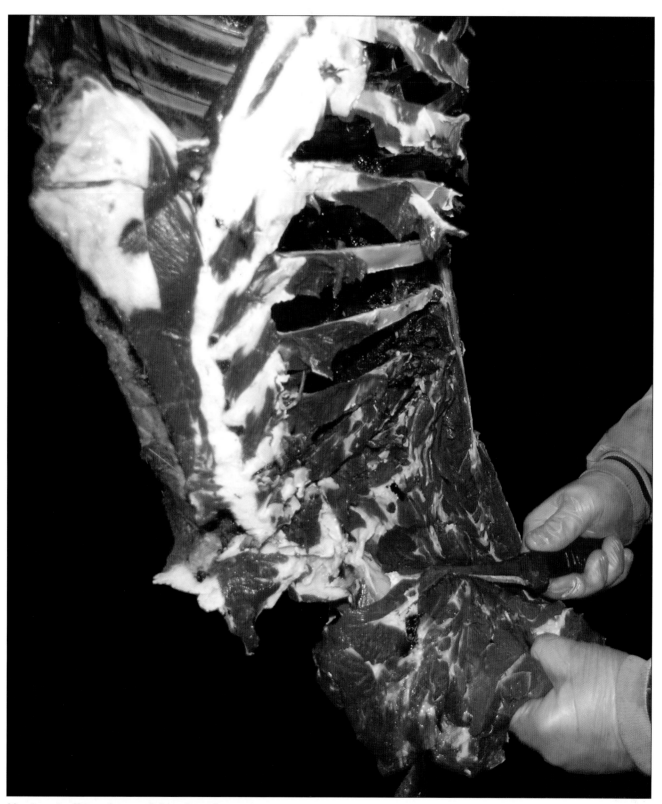

Next, cut off two large slabs of neck meat.

This time around, we'll start working on the neck while the carcass is still hanging. Later, we'll finish up with a little more trimming at the bench.

To get started, simply continue with the two "inner" cuts you made to remove the backstraps. Extend these cuts along either side of the spine, all the way to where you removed the head.

As you proceed along the neck, carefully work your blade between the meat and the vertebrae. Then fillet downward alongside the neck. If all goes well, you'll be able to remove a single slab of meat from either side of the neck.

These chunks make great slow-cooker roasts; they also work well for stew, burgers or sausage. Either way, you'll want to trim away as much fat and connective tissue as possible. Be certain to remove the large yellow tendons on either side of the neck.

By now, you've removed most of the meat from the rib cage and neck. You may, however, still be able to whittle away another pound or two for your burger bucket. That job will be easier over at the bench; let's separate the rib cage and neck from the hindquarters.

Separate the Rib Cage and Neck From the Hindquarters

This step goes quickly. To separate the rib cage and neck from the hindquarters, simply use your knife to slice between two vertebrae. You won't cut bone; you'll only cut the disc and the spinal cord. Choose the first space below the point where the "V" of the hindquarters meets the spinal column.

Slice through the disk between these two vertebrae. Rather than dulling your knife, stop when you reach bone; that's the curve of the vertebra.

Now bend the lower portion of the carcass backward. The rib cage and neck may simply snap free at this point. Or, you may still need

By now, you've removed most of the meat from the rib cage and neck.

Here's where to separate the rib cage and neck from the hindquarters.

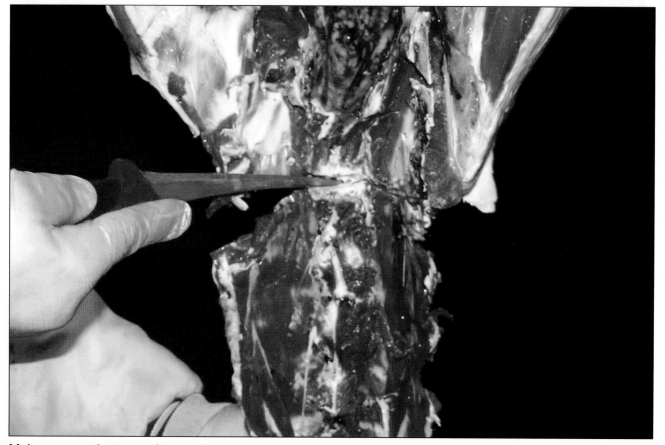

Make your cut between the vertebrae.

to cut through the spinal cord and a little bit of connective tissue. Once you do that, this piece will be free.

If you already trimmed all the meat you want from the ribs and neck, you can put this piece in your scrap tub. If not, take it over to the bench for a few more minutes of whittling.

Continue Trimming the Rib Cage and Neck

Even if you already trimmed the ribs and neck, you may be able to whittle a few more pounds of meat from various nooks and crannies. As you do, take time to trim away as much fat, connective tissue and silverskin as possible.

A commercial processor wouldn't take nearly as much time here, but you can. We won't preach; you can make your own decisions about how much gristle you want to trim out, how much meat you're willing to lose, and how much time you want to spend recovering those last few ounces of stew meat. It's your call.

Bend the neck and rib cage backward to snap them free.

CHAPTER 11

Butchering The Hindquarters

This has been quite a job. Now, finally, the end is in sight.

The hindquarters will have a lot of meat on them. Most of it will be prime steaks and roasts, with a few scraps and various bits for your burger bucket.

Take the Hindquarters Down From the Gambrel

First, take the hindquarters down from the table and carry them over to your bench. Then trim away any areas that are dirty, crusted or dried.

In the next photo, you can see that we split the pelvis during field dressing. (If we'd waited, we might have exposed less of the hindquarters to this kind of drying or contamination.) If

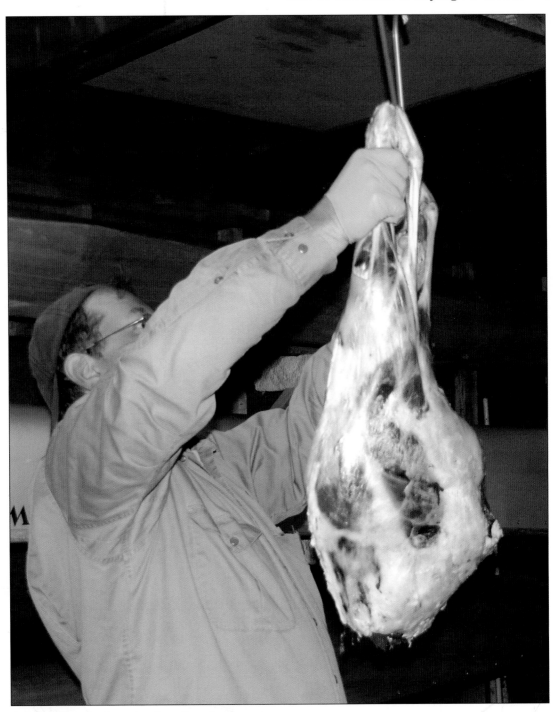

Careful! They're heavier than they look.

Trim away any areas that are dirty, crusted or dried.

you haven't already split the pelvis, that's okay. There's no need to do so now.

Separate the Hindquarters from the Pelvis

Next, lay the hindquarters down with the legs facing you. The area where the tail used to be should now be toward the table.

Right where the pelvis meets the leg, begin cutting downward, with the blade of your knife running right alongside the pelvic bone. As you slice downward, the meat will naturally pull outward and away from the bone. By the time you cut about halfway through, you'll reveal the ball-and-socket joint that attaches the rear leg to the pelvis.

Next, cut carefully through the connective tissue that holds the joint together; when you do, the two pieces will fall apart almost effortlessly. This joint is surrounded by heavy cartilage; even if you're cutting in exactly the right spot, you'll still encounter some resistance. But if the edge of your blade is actually hitting bone, try moving your knife a little one side or the other. When you find a spot where there's less resistance you'll know you've found the joint.

Once you've cut through the joint, it will fall open most of the way. Still remaining, however,

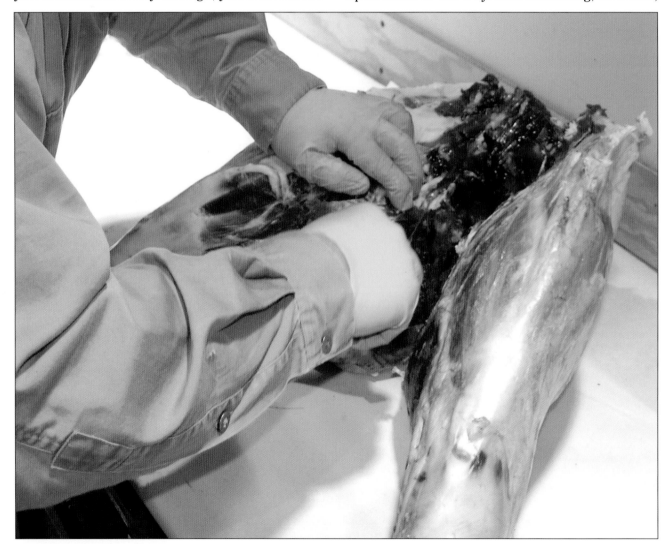

To separate the hindquarters from the pelvis, begin cutting here.

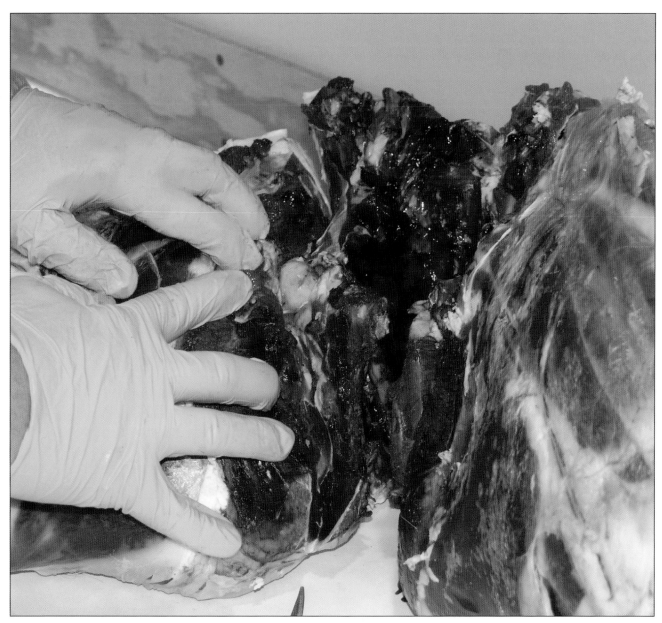

Next, cut through the joint.

will be a heavy tendon that runs adjacent to the joint. After you cut this tendon, you'll feel the leg spring away from the pelvis even more.

By now these two pieces will be almost completely separated. You've cut through the joint, and can now continue the downward cut you were making when you encountered the ball-and-socket joint.

This cut is a little tricky; fillet alongside the bone, following some irregular contours. You'll end up with one or two medium-sized, irregularly shaped pieces for your burger bucket. In a moment you can trim off any pieces you missed.

Now, in a similar fashion, separate the other rear leg from the pelvis. Set the two hindquarters aside for a moment while you finish trimming the remaining scraps of meat from the pelvis. These pieces can go straight into your burger bucket.

Once you've trimmed most of the meat off the pelvis, set it aside in the tub reserved for leftover bones and scraps. Now it's time to debone the hindquarters.

Debone the Hindquarters

During this step you'll focus on the upper portion of the leg. That's where most of the meat is.

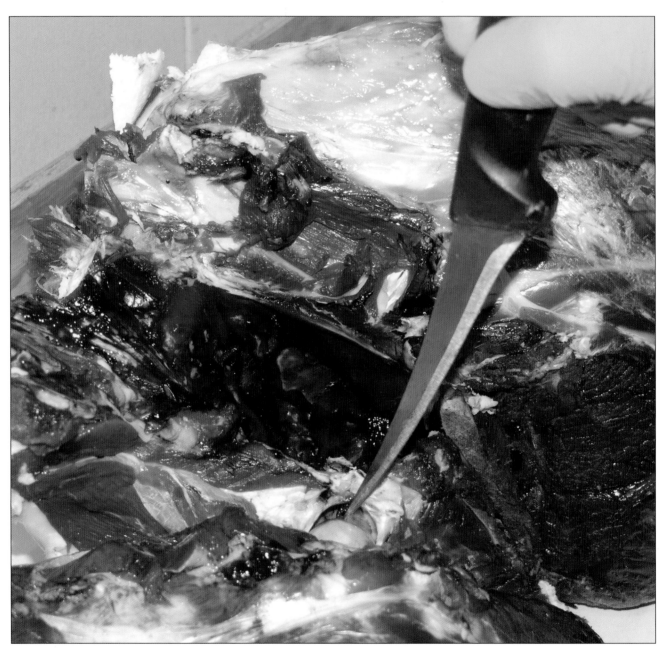

When you cut this tendon, you'll see the ball and socket open right up.

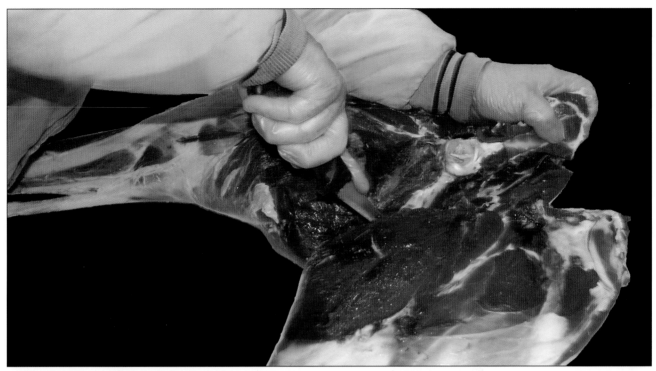

After you're through the joint, continue cutting downward alongside the pelvis.

Now separate the other rear leg from the pelvis.

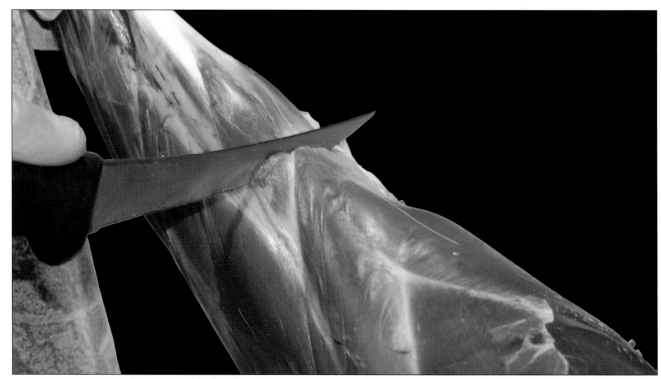

Here's where you'll make your first cut.

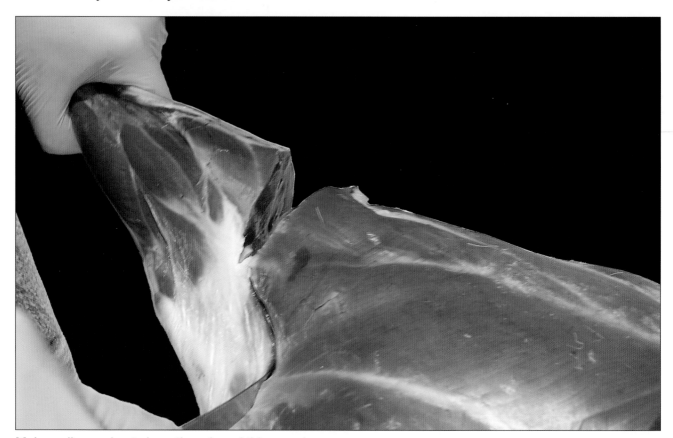

Make a diagonal cut along the edge of this muscle group.

The lower part of the leg contains lots of connective tissue but very little meat.

Here's how to find the exact location of your first cut. If you look closely at the back side of either back leg, you'll see where two muscle groups come together. The upper muscle tapers to a point that fits between the upper ends of two muscles extending farther down the leg. You'll make your first cut right at the point of the upper muscle.

Cut straight in, but don't use a lot of pressure. Ideally, you'll cut all the way down to the bone without dulling your knife by actually cutting against the bone. Then extend the cut for another inch or so on both the inner and outer sides of the leg.

Next, make a diagonal cut upward and toward the front, just along the edge of this muscle group. Then do the same thing on the other side. For now, don't cut all the way around.

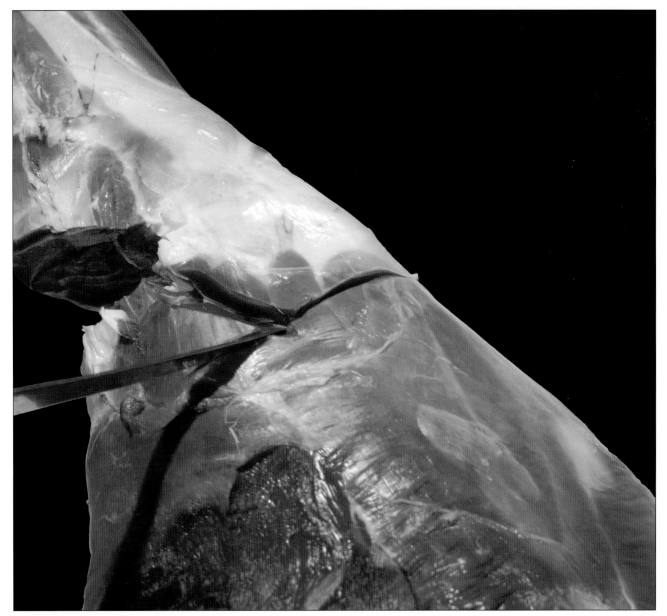

Now make another horizontal cut on the front side of the leg.

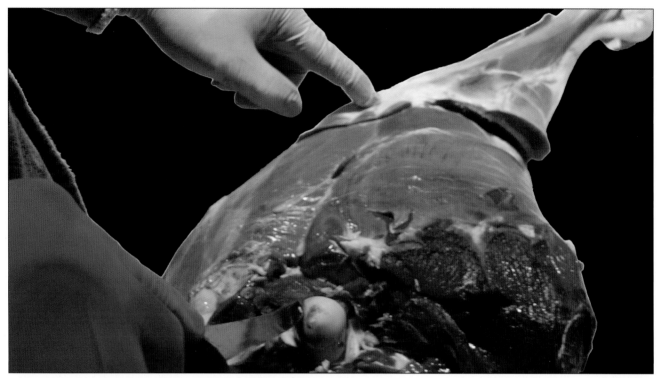

Next, make a diagonal cut along this imaginary line.

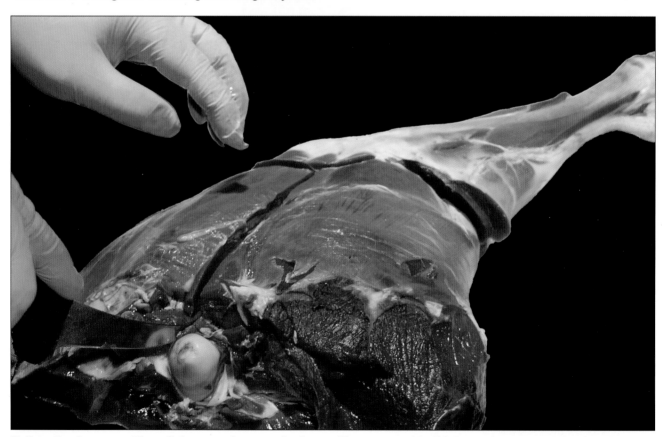

Follow the femur, cutting all the way down to the bone. The exposed ball joint makes a great landmark.

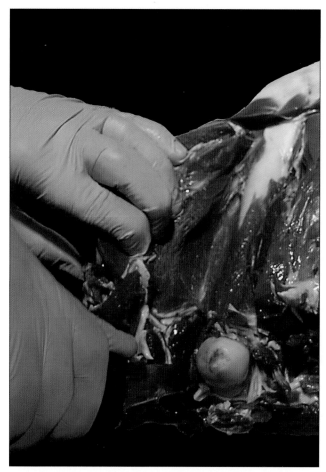

Work your knife along the other side of the bone.

Instead, make another horizontal cut on the front side of the leg. You'll make this cut immediately above the joint. Extend it a short distance around the inner and outer sides, just as you did with the other cuts. You've now cut all the way around the leg.

If you haven't cut to the bone, make a second pass with your knife. Better to make a second pass than to dull your knife by pressing too firmly the first time around.

You now have a large, slightly tapered cylinder of venison that's totally free at both ends. Unfortunately, it's still firmly attached to the femur; we'll take care of that next.

Position the rear leg on your bench so its inner side is facing upward. Look into the cut you've just made; if you look closely, you'll be

You're getting there.

able to see where the femur is connected to the lower leg. Now imagine a diagonal line that runs straight from there to the ball that used to be part of the ball-and-socket joint. That's where the femur is.

Next, make a diagonal cut along this imaginary line. Cut down through the meat, all the way down to the bone. Again, cut more gently when

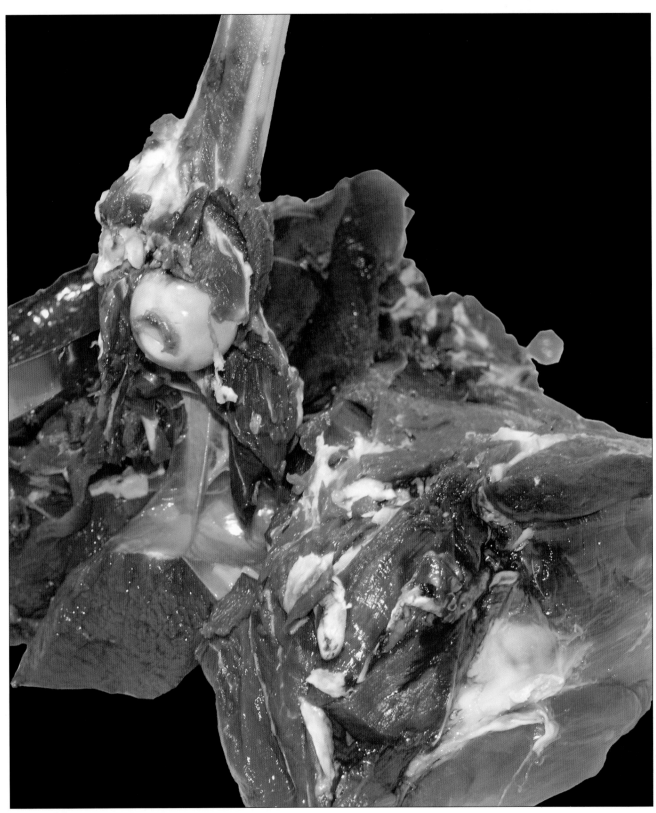

Your steaks and roasts are freed from the femur.

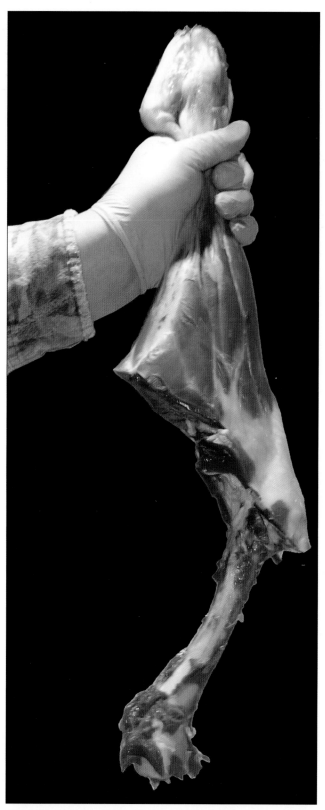

There's still a small amount of meat left on the lower leg.

you get closer to the bone. It takes a while to get the feel of this; with experience, you won't need to sharpen your knives quite so often.

We usually start from the lower end and cut toward the ball end of the femur. You could also start at the opposite end; after you've got a good sense of the femur's location either direction works fine. But when you're doing this the first few times it's easier to stay on track if you use that exposed ball joint as a landmark.

Once you've reached the femur, work your knife along either side of the bone. This is a little tricky, especially when you're just beginning to widen your cut; carefully fillet along the length of the bone without dulling your knife by cutting against the bone. Don't worry if you leave a few scraps of meat adhering to the femur; you can always trim them off later.

Next, use small, shallow cuts to free the meat along the other side of the bone. The meat will be firmly attached all the way along the length of the bone; this is one of those times when you won't be able to just pull and peel. Be patient and take your time.

At times, you may find it easier to hold the hindquarter steady if you pick it up by the lower leg, leaving most of the weight resting on the table. That way, you can position it so the weight of the meat pulling away from the bone will help free it. Continue with short, shallow cuts. Soon the meat will be separated from the bone along most of the femur.

Your progress may be a little slower as you get close to the ball end. You'll encounter more connective tissue plus a few curves that you'll need to trim around. Follow the contour of the bone as best you can.

If a few ounces of meat are still left on the bone, especially in that awkward area up near the ball joint, don't worry about it. Later, trim these scraps off and throw them in your burger bucket.

A bit more trimming around that ball joint,

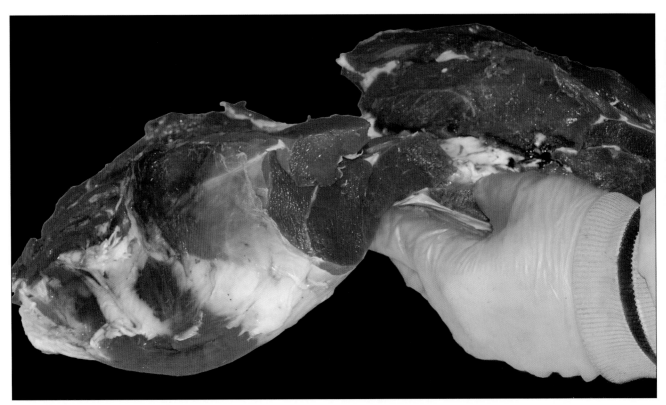

Off the bone and ready for the next steps.

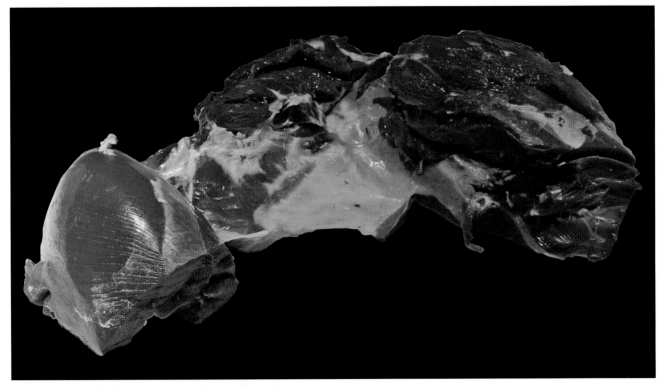

Let's spread all this out to see what we've got.

First, square off the end.

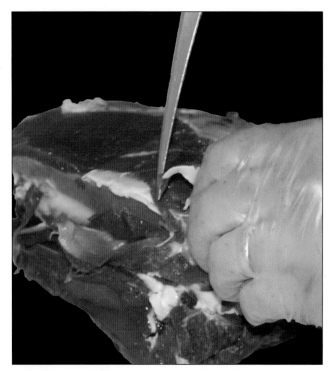

Before we continue, do a little trimming.

and... There! Your steaks and roasts are freed from the femur and you're ready to start carving them up.

Next, depending on how much room you have on your bench, you may want to complete these same steps with the other hindquarter. Or, cut this one into steaks and roasts right away and work on the other one later.

Debone the Lower Portion of the Rear Legs

Meanwhile, if you're working with another person you can ask them to work on deboning the lower portion of the rear legs. But ask nicely; it's a job that can sometimes be a little frustrating. There's not a lot of meat there and it will take some work to get it.

Unfortunately, there's no secret technique that makes this effortless; you'll need to do a lot of whittling for each additional ounce of

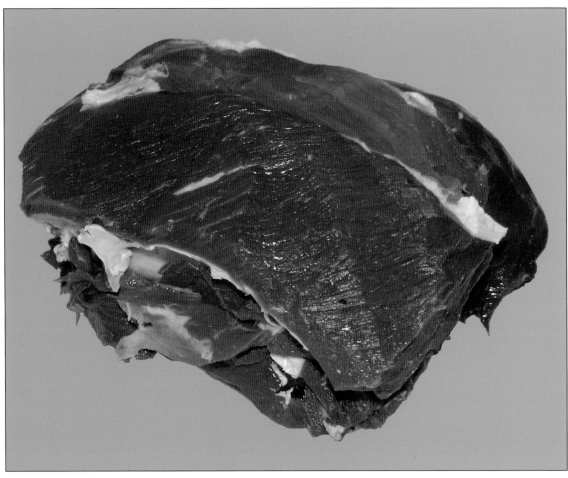

A delicious-looking roast—all trimmed up, with the ends squared off nicely.

deerburger. But since there's more meat here than there was on the same portion of the front legs, it's usually worth the effort.

Cut the Hindquarters into Steaks and Roasts

At this point you have several options. You can turn the hindquarters into roasts and steaks, or some combination of roasts, steaks and hamburger meat. We'll show you an approach that yields both steaks and roasts, plus a few odd bits for your burger bucket. Next time around, feel free to vary those proportions.

Once you remove the meat from the femur,

you'll see meat from several different muscle groups all in a jumbled pile that looks something like the images on page 204.

Next, let's spread all this out to see what we've got. You probably ended up with three main chunks. To keep the terminology simple, we'll call them the slow-cooker roast, burger bits, and prime roasts or steaks.

First, the slow-cooker roast. It's that solid-looking chunk on the left. Because it contains lots of tendons and connective tissue, it works best with a slow, moist recipe. We usually label these packages "roast for slow cooker."

In the center, you'll see a large, irregular piece

Or, you could cut this chunk up into more steaks.

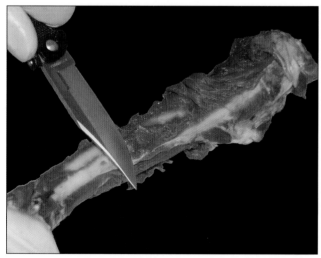

It's almost time to stop.

with lots of connective tissue. You could turn it into steaks or small roasts; they work okay for a slow-cooking recipe. Instead, we usually separate the various muscle groups, trim away any fat and connective tissue, and use the pieces that remain for hamburger, sausage or stew. We'll just call these pieces "burger bits."

We've saved the best for last. The large slab on the right can be turned into several pounds of prime roasts or steaks. First, let's square off the end, being careful to slice across the grain of the meat.

The very first slice will be a bit irregular. We

can either pound it flat with a mallet, cut it into chunks for kebabs, or throw it into the burger bucket. The remaining slices will be nice, symmetrical chunks.

As you cut across the grain of the meat, you'll see that each slice includes a number of different muscle groups. That's okay. Instead of separating them, continue cutting across the grain to make a few steaks.

Or, now that we've squared off the end, we could use the rest for a roast. Either way, pause to trim the fat and connective tissue from the outside of this chunk. Also trim off any areas that are dried or crusted.

In a moment, we'll have a nice slab of boneless meat that contains very little fat or connective tissue. During cooking, the small amount of silverskin between the muscle groups will break down almost completely.

You could leave this as one large roast or cut it into two or three smaller ones. For variety, leave this one as a large roast and make smaller ones from the corresponding portion of the other hindquarter.

Or, you could continue slicing across the grain until you've cut this entire piece into nice, thick slabs of steak. You may even decide to turn one hindquarter into steaks and the other into roasts. It's your call.

Once you've performed these steps with both hindquarters you're nearly done. All that's left is a little more whittling and trimming. Just remind yourself that it's twenty more tacos, twelve more deerburgers, two more pans of lasagna, or…

Eventually, however, you'll reach a point of diminishing returns. The few remaining scraps will be smaller and stringier, and you'll be working harder and harder for every last ounce. Soon it will be time to stop. You'll know when.

What to do With the Remaining Bones and Scraps

It's usually okay to bag up leftover bones and scraps and put them in your regular curbside garbage. In some areas, however, it's possible that garbage companies won't accept them; you may need to personally deliver them to the closest designated landfill.

But if it's legal and if you live in a more rural area (especially if there are coyotes or wolves), you may want to return these leftovers to the wild so they can rejoin the natural cycle. If you do, put them in an out-of-the-way area, far from any homes, roads or trails. If you're not sure, ask around to see what's legal and customary in your area.

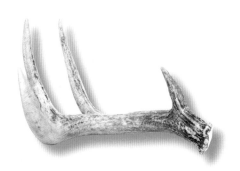

CHAPTER 12

Wrapping and Freezing Your Venison

We recommend paper *and* plastic.

As we noted earlier, you may want to make your packages a little smaller than what you're used to when you buy beef or pork from the grocery store. Your venison is lean meat with no bones or fat. Don't worry, however, if your packages vary in size. That way you'll be able to choose a size that matches your appetite.

Truth in labeling.

Paper or Plastic? Both!

If you wrap and freeze your venison correctly, it will last for a year or more with absolutely no freezer burn and no loss of flavor.

We recommend an inner layer of plastic and then an outer layer of waxed freezer paper. First, wrap the package tightly with plastic wrap; be careful to squeeze out all the air. If you wrap a few extra layers around the package, so much the better. Then wrap the package again with freezer paper.

For better protection against freezer burn, wrap both layers tightly. Finally, use a few bits of freezer tape to seal the packages. This tape looks like masking tape, but it's made to work better at low temperatures.

Label Packages Clearly

Label each package with the date and a description of what's inside. If you know a certain cut is likely to be a little tougher, use labels like "steaks for marinade" or "shoulder roast for slow cooker."

If you process more than one deer in the same session, you may even want to keep some cuts separate and label your packages accordingly. That way you can vary your cooking techniques when you retrieve a package marked "steak from spike buck" rather than one marked "steak from 12 pointer."

Freezing and Thawing Venison

For the best flavor and texture, we recommend that you freeze venison fast and thaw it slowly. To freeze your venison faster:

- **Give your freezer a head start.** Turn your freezer down to its lowest setting before butchering your deer. In a day or two, you can turn it back to its normal setting.

- **Give your venison a head start.** Prechill your venison in the refrigerator before you move it up to the freezer. If it's cold outside you may be able to do this in your garage or out on the porch.

- **Position packages for better freezing.** Leave room for air to circulate. Once all of the packages are frozen solid, stack them however you like.

The way you thaw venison can make a difference too. We recommend thawing it slowly but safely, preferably in the refrigerator. Never defrost your venison in the microwave or by running warm water over the package. Save these techniques for ground beef that you buy after you've run out of ground venison.

VACUUM PACKING SYSTEMS

V acuum packing systems are the best way of all to prevent freezer burn and preserve the flavor of frozen venison. Because they remove all the air from hidden pockets and small irregularities on the outside of the package, they do an especially good job of protecting ground meat from freezer burn. If you plan to be eating deerburgers just before next year's hunting season (and maybe on into the following winter), one of these devices might be worth considering.

You'll also, however, want to weigh all that against the cost of the machine and the ongoing cost of all those bags you'll go through. As with razors and blades, or printers and toner cartridges, it's the cost of those "consumables" that adds up over the long run. And depending on the unit you've purchased, you may find that these devices aren't time-savers at all; your venison may actually take a little longer to package.

If you do buy one of these machines, we suggest you save your money and invest in a good one. It's a lifetime investment, and you'll never be sorry you held out for a better one. Meanwhile, you'll do fine with the "paper and plastic" method. Even once you've bought a vacuum-packing system, you may decide to use a vacuum packer for hamburger, but then use the other, more low-tech method for everything else.

CHAPTER 13

Making Deerburger, Sausage and Jerky

The first time around you may be perfectly satisfied with a freezer full of steaks, roasts and stew meat. Eventually, however, you may want to experiment with deerburger, sausage and jerky—probably in that order.

Grinding Your Own Venison

Quality deerburger starts long before you flip the switch on your grinder. Take time to trim away as much connective tissue as possible. Even if you know you'll be grinding them up later, those gristly bits don't help the texture of your burger.

If you cut venison into smaller chunks your grinder is less likely to jam. You'll also get better results if the meat is chilled or partially frozen—but not, of course, totally frozen.

For us, those partially-frozen chunks are easy to come by. Since we each hope to shoot more than one deer per season, we often freeze the "burger bits" from early-season deer. Then, later in the fall, we thaw them and combine them with the same cuts from a few more deer. That way we're only setting up our grinders once or twice a year. (Even then, set-up and clean-up can take almost as long as the actual grinding.)

If you decide to freeze a batch of burger bits and grind it up later, the quality of your deerburger won't suffer from being thawed, refrozen and thawed again. Just be sure to thaw the meat slowly in your refrigerator.

If you trimmed away most of the fat and connective tissue, the meat that comes out of your grinder will be lean, pure and dark red in color. It's going to look very different from the pale, pink hamburger you're used to seeing at the grocery store.

Some people, however, want their ground

Do you really want this in your hamburger?

Smoking Sausage in "The Outhouse"

venison to look, cook and taste just like ground beef. They increase its fat content by mixing in ground beef, ground pork or even straight beef tallow or pork fat. But why mix your venison with fat from farm animals?

Instead, it's easy to make a few small adjustments to your cooking techniques. We'll tell you more in the next chapter. Please try the techniques we've suggested. If you don't like the results, then go ahead and mix in some beef suet or pork fat.

We're betting, however, that you'll leave it out. In fact, if you live where winters are cold, you may want to leave it out for the woodpeckers and chickadees. They love beef suet. We feel that's a much better use of this particular beef by-product.

Making Your Own Sausage

Even hunters who butcher their own deer usually pay someone else to make their sausage. They see it as a more advanced skill, a secret art that's also a huge amount of work. But if you're curious to give it a try, take it step-by-step:

- **Making bulk sausage.** This is only a small step beyond grinding your own burger. Once you've done that, just mix in spices to make the sort of bulk sausage that's used for pizza toppings and casseroles. Or add a different mix of spices, make patties, and you've got breakfast sausage. You can mix your sausage up by hand or use a special meat mixer.

- **Making sausage in casings.** Ready to graduate from sausage to sausages? After grinding your meat and adding spices, stuff the mixture into casings. This requires a sausage stuffer that's either hand-powered or motorized; some meat grinders are compatible with special stuffing attachments.

CURE IT OR REFRIGERATE IT

Please keep in mind that dehydration alone is not enough to guarantee safe storage without refrigeration. Neither is a curing process that uses only salt. If you make your own jerky, please refrigerate it. Or use a cure like one of those you'd use for sausage. Read the instructions carefully and follow them to the letter.

(Yes, we know that may not be how the pioneers did it. But we also know that a lot of pioneers died from food poisoning.)

- **Smoking and curing your own sausage.** After stuffing your own sausage, you can also smoke and cure it yourself. Home curing mixtures are available from a number of sources; be safe and follow the instructions exactly. Commercial smokers are available in a variety of sizes. Or, you can build your own in a size and configuration that works for you. My home-made smoker has for some reason become known as "The Outhouse."

If you prefer to avoid nitrites, nitrates and all those other additives, you can leave them out of the first two types of sausage. You will, however, need to add them when you're using a low temperature process that involves smoking or dry curing. Without them the sausage wouldn't be safe. At the risk of stating the obvious, preservatives do help preserve foods.

There's one more thing that I add to all venison sausage. Despite what we told you a moment ago about not adding fat to ground venison, sausage is a different matter entirely. To get the proper texture, you'll need to mix in some additional fat. Simplest is just plain ground pork, mixed in with ground venison (adding between 20 and 50 percent pork works well). I've also achieved good results by mixing in around 10 to 20 percent straight beef fat or pork fat.

Whole books have been written on the subject of sausage making; if you decide to try smoking and curing your own, you'll definitely want to learn more. It's work, but it's fun. Think of it as a slightly more carnivorous counterpart to making your own pasta or baking your own bread.

Making Jerky

Making jerky is a great excuse to buy special gadgets like choppers, shooters, squirters and dehydrators. As usual, however, you can give it a try without the extra equipment.

Jerky for Beginners

CHOOSING A MEAT GRINDER

Sooner or later, you'll probably want to invest in a meat grinder. When you do, we'd again like to suggest that you wait and invest in a good one. When you're completing these final steps of the deer disassembly process, it will probably be late, and you'll probably be tired.

Or, maybe you've decided to freeze your early-season burger bits in the hopes that you'll get another deer or two later in the fall. Then it turns out that one of those other deer is an old, tough buck; you decide to turn everything but the backstraps into deerburger. On some Saturday in November or December, you may find yourself grinding up a hundred or more pounds of deerburger during a single session.

Either way, you won't want the frustration of a cheap, underpowered grinder that clogs, smokes, groans, and makes the whole job last twice as long as it should. This is one of those times when it pays to invest in quality.

A few pages back, we wrote about the benefits of vaccuum packers—especially if you'll be freezing a lot of ground venison. So which comes first, the grinder or the vacuum packer? As you're budgeting for these purchases, your priorities may be different from ours. But we suggest springing for a good grinder first. If the vacuum packing system has to wait until next year or the year after that, it's OK.

With the "paper and plastic" method we've shown you, your venison—even ground venison—will keep in the freezer just fine for a year or more, with no freezer burn and no loss of flavor. But without a grinder, you'll be using most of those lumps, chunks, and more "highly textured" pieces in stew. And after you've disassembled your first deer or two, you may decide that you still really enjoy stew—just not quite so often.

For a very small initial investment, you could start out with a hand-cranked grinder. They're simple, and there's not a lot to go wrong. The only problem is that you'll need to do lots of cranking to grind up even a modest amount of venison. Even if you keep the blades extremely sharp, it's going to be a tough job.

At the next step up, you'll find a wide variety of light-duty motorized grinders. Most, however, are meant for occasional kitchen use. They're great if you need to grind two pounds of walnuts for a big batch of cookies. They're not so great if you need to grind up 50 or 100 pounds of venison.

We suggest you avoid these grinders altogether. You get what you pay for; ultimately, buying an inexpensive grinder could turn out to be penny wise and dollar foolish. We know people who bought grinders like these and had them fail before making it through the very first deer.

Cheap grinders can also clog more easily, and their motors just aren't up to the job. Because it's so lean, venison takes a little more horsepower to grind. In fact, maybe it's a good rule of thumb to go for a grinder that's rated by horsepower rather than by wattage.

There are a few less expensive alternatives that may be worth considering; if you already own a high-end countertop mixer, then you may be able to find a compatible attachment. Or, if you're mechanically inclined, you could attach a motor to a hand-cranked model. Few do-it-yourself alternatives, however, will ever be as safe or easy to use as a good commercial grinder.

Shop carefully; compare more than just the horsepower ratings. Look for a solid transmission, a loading hopper that's safe and easy to use, and compatibility with attachments like meat mixers and sausage stuffers. Some grinders even have a reverse gear that makes it easier to clear clogs. If you buy a good one, however, that's one feature you may never need.

For a top-quality commercial grinder, you'll probably need to spend two or three hundred dollars. But unless you're grinding venison from more than three or four deer per year, you probably won't need to spend more still on a larger, more powerful model. Consider this a lifetime investment, one you'll never regret.

When you're experimenting with jerky the first time, simply cut pieces from the hindquarters into long, thin strips. Slice them with the grain, or else across the grain diagonally. Marinade these strips in a solution made from ingredients like soy sauce, brown sugar, and onion or garlic powder.

Meanwhile, set your oven to its lowest temperature and move its rack to the highest position. Then put a foil-lined cookie sheet in the bottom of your oven to catch any drippings. Finally, pierce the end of the strips with a toothpick and hang them in the oven. When they're dry, they're done.

With a "jerky shooter" you can make good jerky from ground venison. Otherwise, use tender cuts that don't include a lot of connective tissue. Before you slice up your jerky, carefully remove every last bit of silverskin and fat.

I know one connoisseur who makes jerky from wafer-thin slices of backstrap. Imagine translucent, potato-chip sized pieces of perfect, melt-in-your-mouth jerky. Although I prefer to reserve backstraps for the grill or the pan, that was definitely the best jerky I've ever tasted.

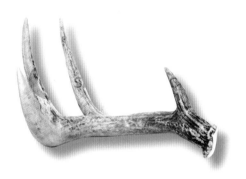

CHAPTER 14

Cooking Your Venison

We haven't padded this book with dozens of recipes. After all, there are plenty of good cookbooks out there. Still, we'd like to offer a few tips. You put a lot of work into your venison; we'd hate to see it ruined in the kitchen.

Why Cooking Venison is Different From Cooking Beef

Venison is leaner than beef.

That's the biggest difference. True, there are subtle differences in the muscle fibers. We've also shown you how to cut your venison into boneless cuts that are different from the cuts of beef you'd buy at the grocery store. The biggest difference, however, is simply that venison is much leaner than beef.

Every deer is different. Some carry a fair amount of subcutaneous and intermuscular fat;

we've suggested, however, that you trim that fat away and discard it. But there's one place you'll never find much fat on any deer—marbled right into the meat itself.

It's this marbled-in fat that makes other meats "juicy." True, some meats from the grocery store contain injected water or marinades; that's especially likely for certain hams and packaged pork products. Usually, however, "juiciness" is all about fattiness.

This doesn't mean venison has to be drier or tougher just because it's leaner. It just means that you'll want to take these differences into

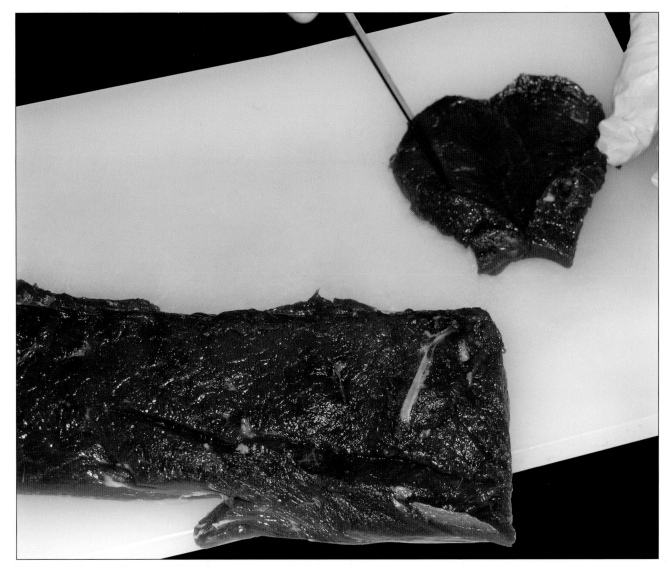

Venison is leaner than most beef.

account and adapt your cooking techniques accordingly.

Most important of all? Don't overcook your venison.

Ground Venison is Different From Ground Beef

Fat doesn't just make meat juicy; it also makes ground beef or pork stick together nicely in a patty or meatloaf. Not to worry. Here's how to adapt your cooking techniques to the lower fat content of ground venison:

- **Burgers on the grill.** Pack your patties tightly. Grill them on a hot flame to sear in the juices. Turn them gently and infrequently—ideally, only once. Be careful to not overcook them.

- **Burgers in a pan.** Again, pack patties tightly and turn them gently and infrequently. And instead of adding fat to your burgers, fry them in a few tablespoons of oil. Olive oil has an especially nice flavor; just be careful to not let it get too hot. If you'd rather not worry about olive oil's low smoking point, use regular cooking oil.

- **Taco meat or sloppy joes (also known as "sloppy does").** First, oil the pan very lightly so your ground venison won't stick when you're browning it. Then brown the meat as usual. When you're done you won't need to pour off extra grease the way you would with ground beef. Instead, pour in a few tablespoons of olive oil. Then add seasonings and stir.

- **Meatloaf.** Use your usual recipe but shorten your cooking time slightly.

Deerburger works great for dishes like spaghetti or lasagna.

For steak, fry it fast and fry it hot. Use a little oil, but not a lot.

You may want to add slightly more moisture in the form of ketchup or barbecue sauce. You can also add more ingredients like diced onions and green peppers; they'll introduce additional moisture as they break down during cooking. If you like, add more egg and breadcrumbs to stretch your recipe; because venison is so lean, your meatloaf will still be plenty meaty.

- **Spaghetti, lasagna and other dishes that use ground meat as an ingredient.** Use your usual recipe with no modification. You'll just end up with a slightly leaner, tastier version. The flavor of venison holds up well in spicy dishes that would overwhelm the flavor of ground beef.

Steaks and Roasts: Cook it Slow or Cook it Fast

Cook it slow or cook it fast. And don't overcook it.

That, in a nutshell, is the secret to perfect steaks and roasts. Slow and moist recipes work great, quick grilling or searing on high heat works great, and anything in between is probably going to be, well, less great.

Again, because venison is so lean it cooks faster than other meats. If you overcook it, it's going to be dry. For the same reason, venison also cools faster than other meats. We suggest you pre-warm your plates and save your salad course for later.

Marinades can be a big help for cuts that are less tender. You can buy them by the bottle or

For roasts, moist, slow recipes work best.

invent your own. Try using beer, buttermilk, wine, Worchester sauce, or grandma's secret recipe.

Sprinkle-on meat tenderizers are also worth a try; for venison, I've generally found the bromelain-based brands work better than papain-based brands. You can also tenderize venison with a meat mallet or various pointy gadgets. Or, save those cuts for stew.

Fry It

The secret to a perfect pan-fried steak is simple. Fry it fast and fry it hot. Use a little oil, but not a lot.

Just a tablespoon or so of oil will be enough to keep your venison from sticking. If you use more oil because you're frying up mushrooms and onions to go with your steak, fry them first and remove them from the pan. Pour out all the oil; whatever's left coating the bottom of the pan will be enough. Then fry your steaks, adding the mushrooms and onions back in just before your steaks are done.

As usual, be careful to not overcook your venison. Take it out of the pan just before you think it's done, and it will probably be about right. Try to poke a minimal number of "test holes;" that way you won't let out all the juices.

If you're pan-frying a thicker piece of venison, start by searing both sides to seal in the juices. Then lower the heat for more even cooking. For thinner steaks or a stir-fry, flash-fry your venison at high temperatures in a minimal amount of oil. Wait until all of your other dishes are ready; this will only take a few seconds.

Grill It

Because venison steaks are so lean, it's especially easy to overcook them on the grill. Give them your full attention. This will only take a moment; you can visit more with your guests later.

Grill thin steaks quickly over a hot flame. Thicker steaks can be done more slowly, but begin with high heat to sear in flavor and juices. To avoid losing those juices, use tongs rather than a fork.

Remove steaks from the grill when they're medium-rare; then serve them immediately. You may want to suggest that your guests save their salads for later. Then again, they may have already decided that for themselves.

For maximum moisture and tenderness, we like to marinade most steaks before grilling them. It's probably not necessary, however, for backstraps. In general, the most prime, tender cuts are probably the ones best suited to grilling.

We've also heard of people grilling an entire hindquarter on a rotisserie, but that's something we haven't tried yet. One of these days…

Roast It

For roasting, our advice would be just the opposite of what we suggested for frying and grilling. We recommend recipes for roasting that

are moist and slow. You can make these half-day and all-day recipes in the oven, but slow cookers are especially convenient.

Some of the tougher cuts respond especially well to this treatment. After long, slow cooking, they can be shredded and used for hot venison sandwiches. Use the same recipes you would for beef sandwiches; shortcut versions involve ingredients like barbecue sauce, onion soup mixes or cream of mushroom soup.

Stew It

On a cold winter's day there's nothing quite like a bubbling pot of stew. It's hot, delicious and makes great leftovers.

Follow the same sort of recipe you'd use when stewing other meats. First brown the venison in a frying pan. Then put it in your slow cooker with all the other ingredients. Wait until later to add spices and seasonings; otherwise the flavors will be lost from prolonged cooking. (Because stovetop recipes require closer supervision, we're big fans of slow cookers. They require more "elapsed" time, but less time in the kitchen.)

In its own way, a hearty venison stew can be just as tasty as grilled backstraps. We like to experiment with different ingredients and seasonings, and we rarely follow a written recipe. Even when we do, every stew somehow tastes a little different. And that's okay.

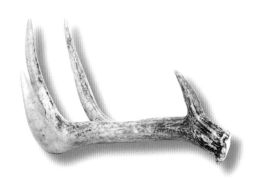

CHAPTER 15

Saving Antlers and Caping Your Trophy

Photo Courtesy Dustin Reid

It's true: You can't eat antlers. Still, we've included this final chapter so you'll know how to:

- Save antlers and create your own wall mount.
- Skin your deer before sending its cape and head to the taxidermist.
- Cape your deer so it's ready for the taxidermist. This involves painstakingly skinning the neck and head without cutting any extra holes through the hide.
- Prepare a European-style mount with a bleached skull and antlers.

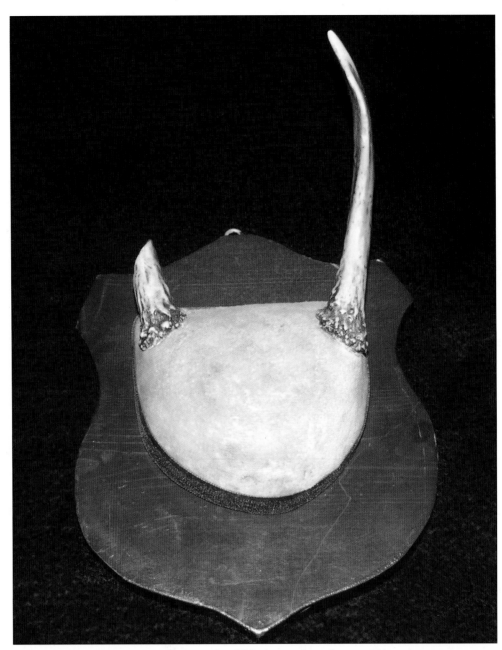

Even beginners can get good results. This is my first deer, a 1½-pointer taken when I was 12 years old.

If you're new to processing venison, you may want to save some of these other projects for later; they're not for the squeamish and they'll require extra skill and patience. Caping involves lots of small, meticulous cuts; the skinning skills you've gained so far are only a warm-up.

We suggest, in fact, that you not wait for the trophy of a lifetime to test your caping skills.

Practice on a few smaller deer. They can be bucks or does; even if you don't plan on sending them to the taxidermist, it's good practice.

If the idea of spending a half-day carefully peeling the skin from a deer's head seems less than appealing, especially if you're doing it just for practice, then you're in good company. Most hunters leave this job to the taxidermist.

If you're on a guided hunt in a remote area, there's also a good chance the outfitter will offer this service.

If you'll be taking the head and antlers to a taxidermist, you can still skin the deer yourself. You'll just need to adjust your technique slightly when you get to the neck.

But simplest, and also least expensive, is saving your deer's antlers for an antlers-only wall mount. We'll tackle that project first.

If You'd Like to Save Just The Antlers

This is the simplest project of all; even beginners can get professional-looking results. The secret is an inexpensive kit that includes a wood plaque with a form, a piece of felt or deerskin to cover the form, and all of the necessary hardware. If you're new to all this, however, there's one small step in this process that you may find a little unpleasant. You're

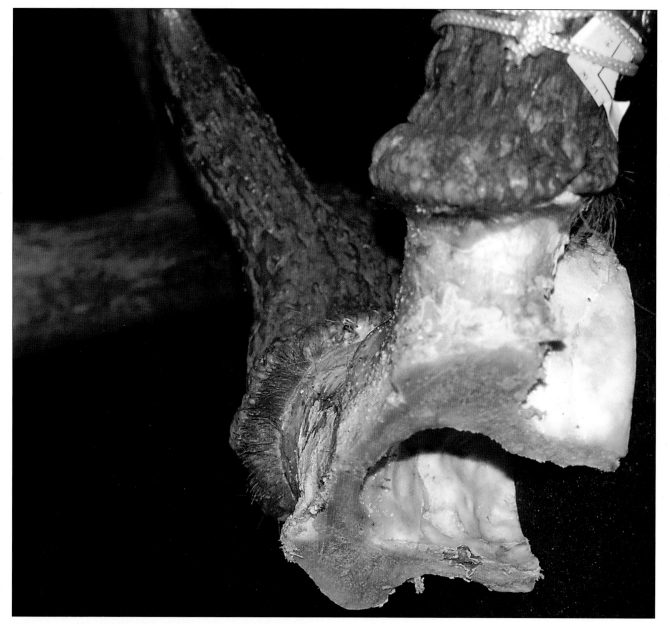

These cuts should form a right angle. Here's one from a few years back.

CONSIDER CWD

You'll be cutting through the deer's skull and into its brain. If you're concerned about CWD, use a blade designated solely for this purpose. Discard it when you're done.

Before you replace the blade, be sure to clean the frame and handle thoroughly. If you're concerned about CWD, soak your saw in a bleach solution for a day or two.

Even if you're not concerned about CWD, you may want to use your hacksaw, discard the blade, and replace it with a new one. The teeth on your old blade could be clogged with bits of skin, hair, and bone. It won't be easy to clean it thoroughly, and hacksaw blades are fairly inexpensive. It might be time to replace your old blade anyway.

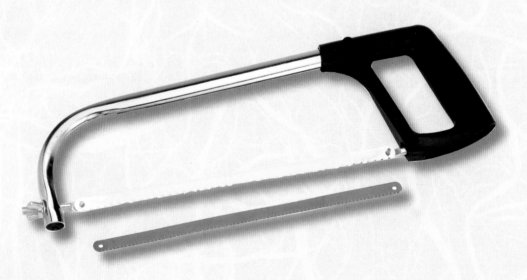

Here's what you'll be delivering to the taxidermist.

CAPES AND CAPING

These terms can be confusing; their meaning varies, depending on the situation. Here's how it works.

Your taxidermist will be happy to work with a head that has a "cape" attached—something like what you see in the photo on page 231. The term "caping," however, is generally used to describe the process of skinning the animal's head.

That's the next step, and it's something that either you or your taxidermist will need to do very carefully with a small, sharp "caping knife." Once this operation is complete, the skin from the head and the front part of the animal is also referred to as a "cape."

Photo courtesy of Brian Goode

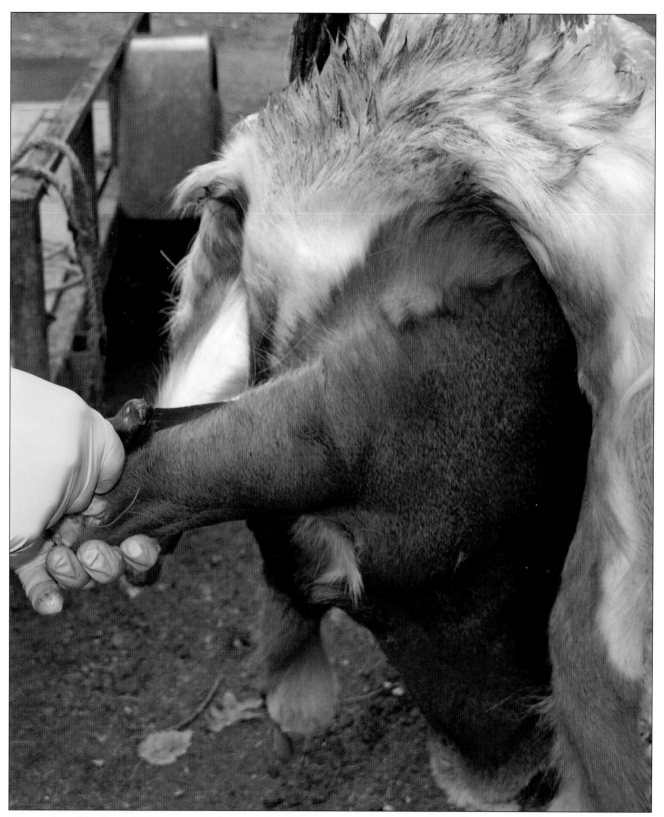

When you skin the front legs, make your cut a bit more to the outside, leaving more white "brisket" fur for your taxidermist to work with.

Continue skinning the neck until you've reached the base of the skull.

Remove the head as you normally would, carefully cutting in between the vertebrae.

going to use a bone saw or a hacksaw to remove a section of the deer's skull.

If you were using the antlers as raw material for lamps, chandeliers, door handles or other handicrafts, you could just saw them off at the base. For that matter, you could even use shed antlers that you've found in the spring. But for a wall mount, you'll need to remove the antlers together, along with a slice of the skull. That way they'll be positioned and aligned correctly in relation to each other.

You'll make two cuts, one from the top and another from the front. Make these cuts at about a 90-degree angle. The front cut should go through the middle of the eye sockets, or else right about at their top edge. If you're not sure how much of the skull to cut out with your antlers, err on the generous side; you can always trim a little off later.

This step will be easier if you first skin the area you'll be cutting through. That way the hair won't clog the teeth of your saw. Do this during the first day or two, before the skin dries and toughens. Rather than procrastinating, get out your saw and get it done.

Next, scrape the skull plate clean. Any remaining skin won't come loose easily; you'll need to scrape it off bit by bit. The good news is that you're not saving this skin so there's no need to keep it in one nice, neat piece. Scrape the skull plate with a dull knife until it's completely clean.

Sometimes a wire brush can be helpful for the last few scraps of connective tissue. Some people boil the skull plate for a while in a solution of bleach and water. If you do, be careful not to get any on the antlers.

Next, salt the skull plate down and let it dry for several weeks. I use the bottom half of a plastic laundry detergent container. It's just the right size, and the plastic is easy to cut. After I cut the top off, I cut two notches for the antlers.

After the first week or so, you'll want to change the salt. By then, it will have already pulled most of the moisture out of skull plate; it's time for some fresh, dry salt. Then, after a few more weeks have gone by, the skull will be totally dry.

From here on, just follow the instructions that came with your antler mounting kit.

If You'd Like a Head-and-Shoulders Mount, But Don't Want to Do Your Own Caping

An antlers-only mount is a relatively simple do-it-yourself project. A full head-and-shoulders mount, however, is the sort of job you'll probably want to leave to a professional. If you can deliver a head with the cape attached, your taxidermist will take it from there.

This project involves very little extra work on your part; you'll just be performing certain steps a little differently. Most of those steps come during the final moments of the skinning process.

Until then, there are really only two differences. When you're field-dressing your deer, stop at the sternum. Don't cut any farther. (You might not anyway; now, however, this becomes especially important.) And, when you get your deer home leave its head on. You'll remove it later when you're done skinning your deer.

A deflated deer. The head and skin are ready for your taxidermist.

If you'd like to trim off the rear portion of the hide, use a straight edge to guide your cut.

Before you leave for your hunt, you may want to ask your local taxidermist for any special instructions. Most taxidermists will be very happy, however, if you follow the instructions on the next few pages.

They'll be especially grateful if you:

- Don't cut your deer's throat during field dressing.

- Don't drag your deer out of the woods for a mile or two over rocks and brush and then expect your taxidermist to repair the damage.

- Don't drag or hang your deer with a rope around its neck. If you must drag your deer, don't drag it backwards for even a short distance.

- Get your deer's head and cape to the taxidermist as soon as possible; this is especially important in warm weather. If it's warm, ice the head and cape but keep them dry.

- Leave plenty of hide attached to the head; taxidermists can always trim some off, but they can't add more back on.

With that last point firmly in mind, you may even want to deliver the entire skin to your taxidermist. It won't make your job any harder. But if you do choose to cut away the rear portion of the hide, you can do so when all the skinning is done.

Skin your deer just as you normally would, with only a few small variations as you reach the neck and shoulder area. First, follow a slightly different route as you skin the front legs. Cut farther to the outside; so your taxidermist will have more white "brisket" fur to work with.

Carefully skin the brisket flap down toward the neck. Leave a larger flap than usual; this "armpit" area will be included on your mount.

Now skin the neck in the usual fashion. As you get closer to the head, roll the neck hide inside-out, closer and closer to the skull. As we mentioned earlier, the neck can be one of the more difficult parts of a deer to skin, especially on an older buck. But if you can, continue until you reach the base of the skull.

Some people, however, prefer to go as far as they can and then make a neat, careful slit along the back of the neck. If you do this, cut from the inside, starting near the head and cutting with the grain of the hair. (To better visualize this, check out the photos that show the first few steps of the caping process.)

This will give you more maneuvering room, and it's something your taxidermist will need to do later anyway. Once your deer is up on the wall, the back of its neck will be toward the wall and the ceiling. Any repairs in that area will be less visible.

Don't, however, make any cuts along the throat or the front of the neck. Even for the best taxidermists, these cuts are difficult or impossible to hide.

If you can, however, it's best to continue until you've reached the base of the skull. Take your time and be patient. This stretch can be slow going, and any mistakes could be tough for your taxidermist to conceal.

Next, remove the head as you normally would, carefully cutting in between the vertebrae. Use special caution during this step; it's easy to cut through the hide if you're not careful.

Turn the hide fur side-out, spread the head

and cape out on the ground, and roll it up for your taxidermist. If you'd like to remove the rear portion of the hide and deliver a smaller bundle, now's the time. It's easiest to hold the hide down with a straight edge that you can use to guide your cut. Again, leave plenty; err on the side of caution.

Get the head and cape to your taxidermist quickly. Keep them cold or frozen; if you can't, salt them heavily. Salt is cheap. Use lots.

If you're traveling, change salt periodically. That way the fresh, dry salt can continue pulling moisture out of the head and cape. If the skin begins to spoil, the hairs will come loose and the cape will be ruined. (When this happens, taxidermists sometimes speak of the hair "slipping." It's not a good thing.)

If You'd Like a Head-and-Shoulders Mount, and You're Ready to Cape Your Own

Caping isn't easy. Still, there are some good reasons to someday give it a try.

Some hunters do their own caping so they can sell the cape to a taxidermist. In a pinch, taxidermists can use these raw materials to replace damaged capes they've received from their customers. Or, they can use them to make mounts for sale to local taverns and restaurants.

Here's where you'll poke your knife through from the inside.

Reach in with your caping knife to cut from the inside. That way, you'll be able to slit the skin without cutting the hairs.

And, as we noted earlier, there may be situations when you won't have any choice but to do your own caping. If you're hunting without a guide or in a remote area where you'll need to fly your trophy out or carry it out on your back, then you'd better be ready to cape your own.

Most hunters who tackle this project, however, just try it for the extra challenge. And it is a challenge. We want to be positive and encouraging; we also, however, want you to go into this with realistic expectations.

As we've mentioned, the skin on a deer's head tends to hang on tight. And if you slip up, it could be tough for your taxidermist to hide the damage—damage that will probably be in an area where it's especially visible.

Even if your work is flawless, you shouldn't expect that your taxidermy bill will be lower because you've tackled this part of the job. For taxidermists, this is only the first step in a long process. If they need to make extra repairs, your bill could actually be a little higher.

Get in some practice ahead of time. Don't wait for the trophy of a lifetime, and don't wait until you're out in the bush somewhere with flies buzzing around your head and a grizzly bear with half-grown cubs likely to wander by at any moment.

Instead, practice on a few "ordinary" deer, back home at the workbench in your own garage.

Work in an area that's comfortable and well-lighted. Make sure you've got plenty of room and that your work surface is at a comfortable height. The first time you do this, it's going to take at least an hour or two.

Even after you've done this a few times, it takes a while. But it's not a race. Work slowly and methodically. Think carefully about what you're hoping to accomplish with each cut you make. Think first and cut second.

Here's one final detail. If a few small areas are partially frozen, you may be okay. But it's just about impossible to cape a head that's entirely frozen. If it's too warm, on the other hand, some areas will be softer and more flexible; that means it's tougher to make precise cuts. Cold or cool is just right.

If we still haven't managed to discourage you from trying this, then let's get started. You've separated the head and cape from the rest of the deer; let's assume that you've removed the head right at the base of the skull.

At this point you won't be far from the antlers. To reach them, cut forward a little farther, skinning upward along the back of the deer's head. When it becomes difficult to make further

Slowly and carefully, pull toward the rear.

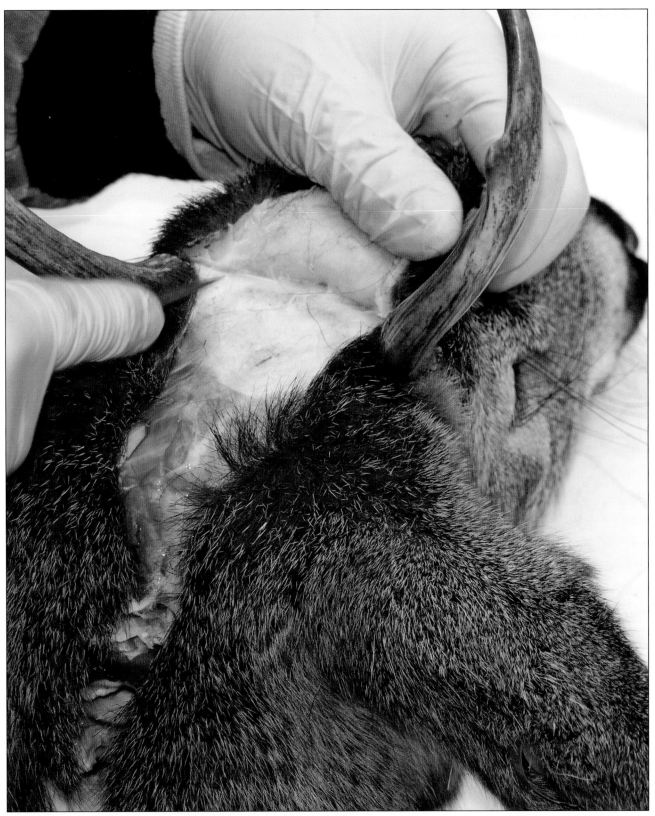

Next, make similar cuts from the base of both antlers. Make a cut from each antler to the cut you made at the base of the neck. You'll be able to lift a v-shaped flap.

progress, you'll be at the back of the skull, just a little behind the antlers.

Here, you'll reach in with your caping knife to cut from the inside. That way you won't cut any hairs. Reach in with your knife as far as you can—ideally, until you're even with the base of the antlers. The carefully cut upward and outward; make a single cut toward the rear, slitting the cape all the way along the back. Continue until you're past the shoulders and you've slit the cape along its entire length.

Next, make similar cuts from the base of both antlers. Then cut around the antlers, being careful to not cut through any of the hairs at

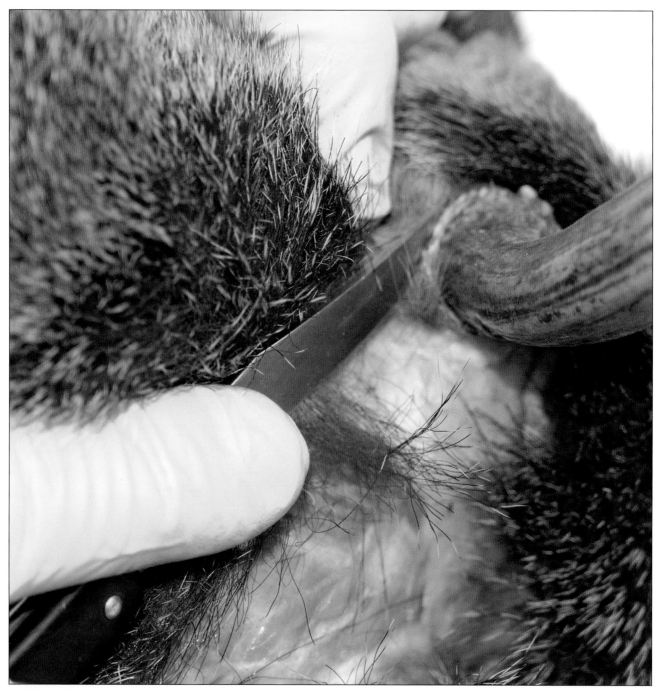

Work slowly and carefully around the antlers.

the base. To loosen the skin around the base of the antlers, you may need to do a little prying. Sometimes a flat-bladed screwdriver works well for this step. Or, dig a little deeper into your toolbox for a pliers, and maybe even a visegrip.

Along the back of the head, make a short cut downward on both sides. These cuts should only extend downward two or three inches from the cut you've made along the back of the neck. Longer cuts will make the rest of the job easier, but shorter cuts will be less visible and easier for your taxidermist to sew back up.

From here on you won't be making any more

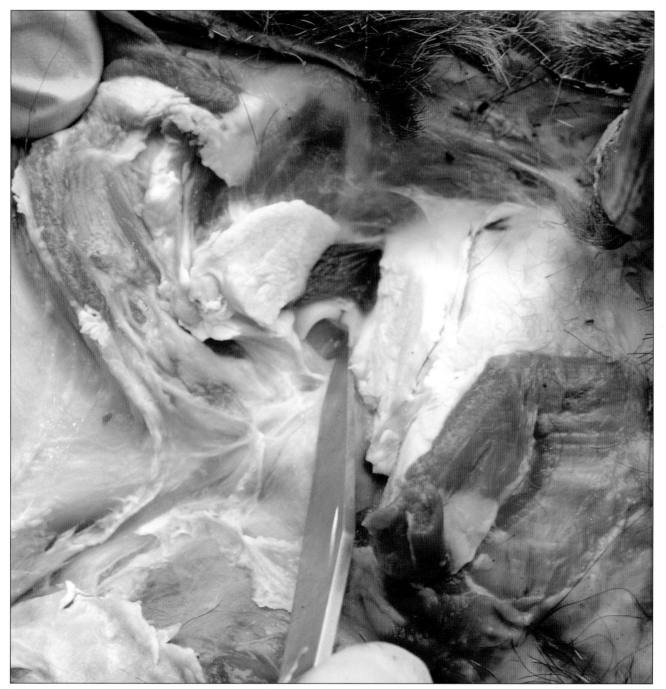

Cut through the ear canal and as close to the skull as possible.

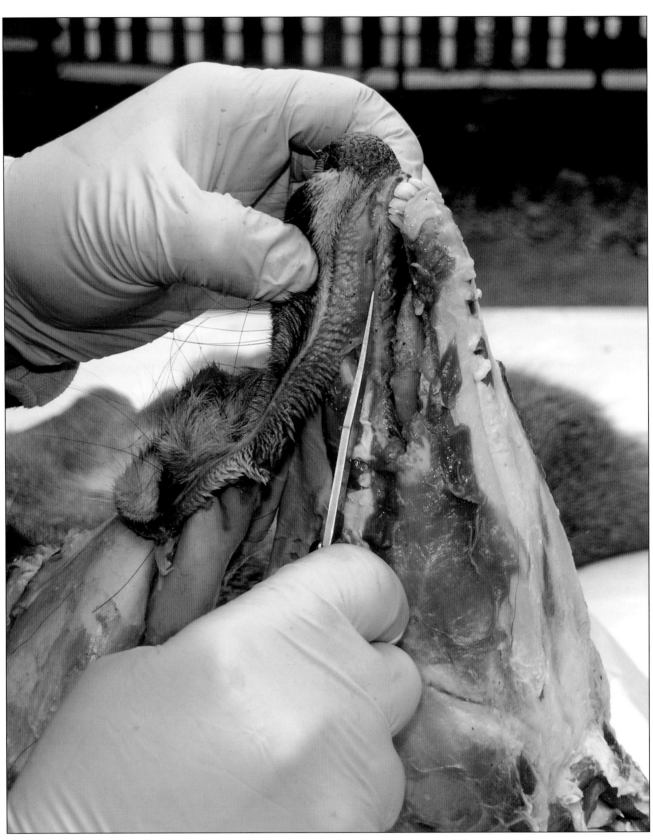

Cut the lips free on the inside of the mouth, as close to the gumline as possible.

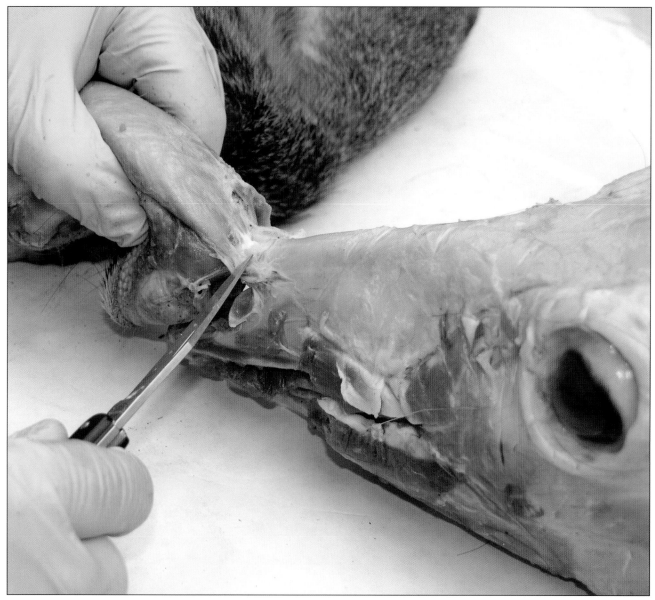

Leave as much nose cartilage attached to the cape as possible.

slits. You'll only be skinning and peeling. There aren't any easy parts left. But these tips may help:

- **Take your time.** It's not a race. Later, you may be able to finish a caping job in a matter of minutes. The first few times, plan on at least an hour or two.

- **Pause frequently to resharpen your knife.** You'll need a razor edge for every cut you make, and yet it's hard to avoid scraping your blade against the skull.

- **Think of this process as scraping rather than skinning.** When you skin a deer, you cut into the seam that opens up between the skin and the meat. Now, however, you'd rather have your knife angled toward the skull; that's especially true when you're doing this the first few times.

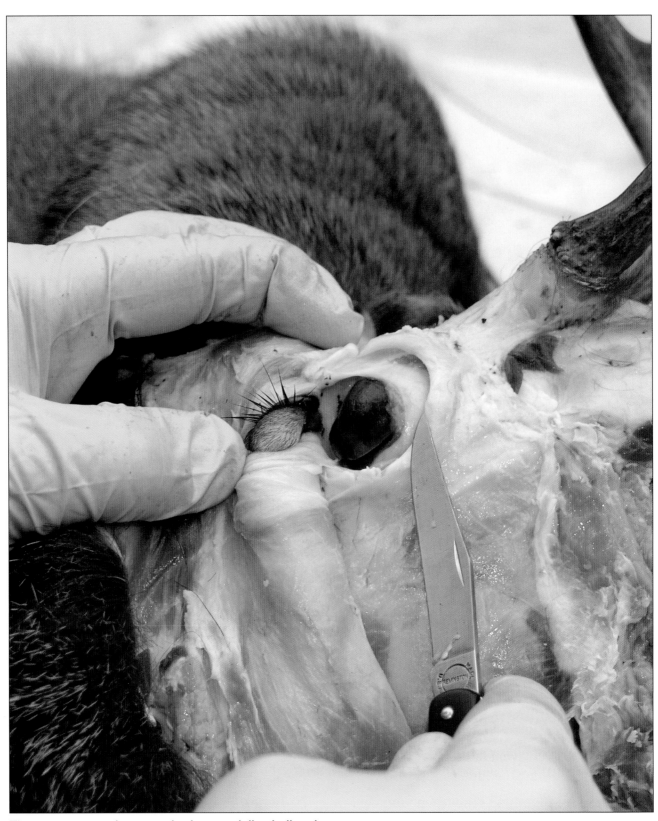

The eyes are another area that's especially challenging.

There's still some work left for your taxidermist.

You're scraping hide away from the skull, and you'd much rather scrape against bone than make extra holes in the hide. Err on the side of caution, even if it means sharpening your knife more often the first few times.

• **Don't worry about leaving extra meat or connective tissue on the inside of the hide.** Your taxidermist can easily remove it later. Don't risk cutting through the hide.

Once you're past the antlers, the next part that's especially challenging will be the ears. You'll want to cut the ear canal as close to the skull as possible; that point is much lower and farther in than you'd expect.

To get a good idea of where the ear canal is positioned, you can stick a finger in it before you make that critical cut with your other hand. Be sure to remove your finger before you continue; then carefully cut through the ear canal as close to the skull as possible.

Later, your taxidermist will remove the cartilage from the ears and replace it with a synthetic insert. This is something you'll probably want to leave to the taxidermist, though. It's easy to ruin an ear, and there are no long hairs to help conceal the repairs.

After you've made it safely past the ears, a little more skinning and peeling will get you to the eyes. This is another area where you'll need to cut very slowly and carefully; pause and resharpen your knife before you continue.

Make sure you leave the inner eyelids attached to the cape; your taxidermist will need them. You'll also want to cut carefully around the tear ducts at the front of the eye. You'll need to cut or pry them out of a small cavity in the skull.

Once past the eyes, you're in the home stretch. Carefully work your way down the nose. When you get to the mouth, reach inside and pull the lips back. Save the lips, and as much of the gum material as you can. Cut right at the gum line.

When you get to the nose, peel it back so you can cut through the cartilage. Cut carefully and leave as much attached to the cape as possible. Your taxidermist can remove the excess later.

Salt the inside of the cape heavily, especially the ears and nose. You can refrigerate the cape for a day or two if necessary, but get it to the taxidermist as quickly as possible. To continue pulling out moisture, start over periodically with fresh, dry salt—especially if you won't be able to keep the cape refrigerated. Salt is cheap; use lots.

Most taxidermists will prefer that you bring them the skull with antlers still attached. That way they can remove the antlers and skull plate in the way that works best for them.

In some cases, of course, this won't be an option. When you're returning from a hunt in an especially remote area, space and weight will be at a premium. You or your guide can saw the antlers and skull plate free, just as you would for an antlers-only mount. Leave plenty of skull plate attached to the antlers; your taxidermist can remove the excess later.

Caping your own trophy is an advanced skill. If you've successfully completed this job, even on a smaller "practice deer," then we salute you. But don't let it go to your head.

This has been some work, and it required extra patience and skill. Now, however, your taxidermist will reunite that limp, salty cape with its antlers and turn it all into an incredibly lifelike wall mount. That requires a whole different set of skills.

The best taxidermists aren't just artisans. They're truly artists. And now, after caping your own deer (or even after just reading about how to do it), you'll better understand why they charge what they do. Maybe those prices aren't so high after all.

If You'd Like to Try a "European" Mount With a Bleached Skull and Antlers

In recent years, these European-style mounts have also become more popular here in North America. Although they're not to everyone's taste, they can have a very classy, elegant look when they're done right.

What's more, even beginners can get good results. I've only experimented with this technique once and it turned out great.

Technically, at least, a European mount is not difficult. There's a reason, however, that I've only done this once. Before you decide to give it a try, you should know that it's a lot of work and that it represents a considerable investment of time. It doesn't take many dollars, but it does take a lot of hours.

It's also a job that can be smelly, messy and not altogether pleasant. You'll be removing the lower jaw and the brain, boiling and scraping the head repeatedly, and then bleaching the skull with strong chemicals. During this process, you'll carefully avoid getting any of those chemicals on the antlers—or, for that matter, on yourself.

If this all sounds a bit much, relax. You can safely turn the page. We haven't illustrated this process with the usual step-by-step series of color photos. We figured that if anyone browsing in a bookstore were to flip to this part of the book first they might assume they were in the recipe section. That would not have been good for sales.

Indeed, the simplest way to describe this project is that it involves several progressively thinner batches of skull soup. First, however, you'll need to remove the lower jaw. Then, using a dull knife, scrape away all of the skin and as much flesh and connective tissue as possible. A pliers and screwdriver may also be helpful, and you'll want to wear some leather gloves that will never be used again for anything else. (Later, during the "skull soup" phase of this project, you'll wear heavy, elbow-length rubber gloves.)

Next, remove the brain. The easiest way to do this is to first remove the lower-rear portion of the skull; later, that portion of the skull can go against the wall plaque. If you'd like the skull to remain intact, you'll need to remove the brain through the eye sockets, bit by bit between boilings.

Nature's version of a European-style mount.

The makings of a European-style mount.

Safety Warning: To protect yourself from the hot water and harsh chemicals, wear heavy, elbow-length rubber gloves during this entire process. And when you grab the skull by the antlers and pull it from the water, be careful. It's going to be full of hot water that will pour out when and where you least expect it.

CWD and Disgusting Backspray Warning: If you've shot a trophy buck in an area where deer are known to be infected with CWD, you may want to consider other taxidermy options. However you may perceive the level of risk that CWD poses to humans, this project involves the risk—or, more realistically, the probability—of repeated, unavoidable contact with numerous small bits of brain and spinal cord. While you're working on this project, we also suggest that you avoid licking your lips.

We've heard of people using a pressure washer to aim a jet of water into the eye sockets, but we'd be a little concerned about the backspray. We also recommend that you not do this with a high-pressure wand at the carwash, no matter how few other people are likely to be there late at night on a Saturday.

Also in the "do not try this at home" category is an alternative skull-cleaning method that's used by some taxidermists. It employs dermestid beetles, and is said to give excellent results.

Don't even think of trying this in the kitchen. Use a camp stove, either outdoors or in a garage with plenty of ventilation. This soup will not smell delicious.

Use plain water, with just a small amount of bleach; too much bleach may soften the skull. Optionally, you can also add a little dish soap to cut the grease. Your goal is to keep the skull fully submerged, but without getting the antlers in the water.

To fine-tune the depth, place a brick or two in the bottom of the pot. Then put the skull in on top of the bricks. Plan ahead; do this before you begin heating the water. If the area near the top of the skull is above the surface, you can ladle some boiling water over that portion every minute or two. Replace the water as it boils away.

After it looks as though the remaining bits of flesh are loosened up, you can pull out the skull, let it cool, and do a little more picking and scraping. Then do it again. And again. Change water occasionally, whenever it looks like it's time.

Prolonged boiling can soften the skull; that's one reason it's better to clean the skull more thoroughly before you begin your sequence of boilings. You may also be able to save yourself some work; a little more scraping in the beginning can save a lot of boiling later.

After a series of boilings, soak the skull for about an hour in hydrogen peroxide, the type that's available in large brown bottles from your local drugstore's health and beauty department. This will bleach it white. If you like, you could also begin the bleaching process earlier, in between boilings. It's up to you.

If teeth or pieces of bone come loose during all of these repeated boilings, don't panic. You'll probably be able to solve the problem with a few drops of superglue.

Keep boiling, soaking and drying the skull until you're absolutely certain there's not a single scrap of tissue or brain anywhere, inside or outside. Once the skull is bleached white, and once it's totally clean and dry, you can spray it with a protective coat of clear acrylic. Then just mount the skull on a wall plaque and you're done.

As an alternative to the household chemicals we've described, you can also use special-purpose chemicals available from a taxidermy supply house. They're a bit stronger and they may give better results. Better yet, order a kit that includes a nicely finished plaque, all the chemicals you need, and detailed, step-by-step instructions.

Why We Hunt

We hope reading about this particular project hasn't ruined your appetite. We, too, find soapy skull soup less than appealing. And, although antlers and trophies can be a great way to remember the hunt, these souvenirs are not by themselves reason enough to hunt.

For most, the challenge of your hunt is reason enough. If you need more reason than that, we'd like to remind you why hunting deer is so challenging in the first place.

There's just one reason deer are so wary and so elusive. It's the reason they've learned to watch their back and watch the wind. It's the reason they've learned to hide so well and run so fast.

Somehow, instinctively, they know…

Venison is delicious.

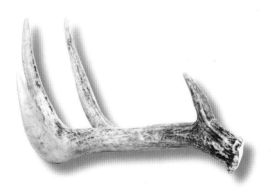

Appendix

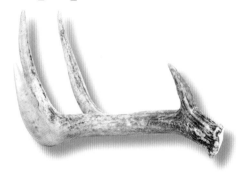

Deer don't have an appendix. If they did, you would already have removed it way back during that chapter on field dressing. You're all done now.

Congratulations on a job well done!

And by the way, we know it's been a lot of work. The first time, it is for everyone. But don't worry. The whole process will be much easier the second time, and easier still the third and fourth time.

So good luck, good hunting and bon appetit!

The One Call That Does It All